DEDICATION

This book is dedicated to every person who has suffered the devastation of sexual sin and specifically to all the women who have ever been the victim in an adulterous relationship.

The heartache of many men and women has gone into the formation of this book. Some were counselees who knew what I was writing and encouraged me and urged me to continue, even as their own lives were in some cases crumbling around their feet as a result of someone else's sexual sin.

May the God of all comfort minister to your heart and soul and strengthen you with His power. May you focus on Jesus Christ and find your joy in Him—even in the midst of suffering.

> *You keep track of all my sorrows.*
> *You have collected all my tears in Your bottle.*
> Psalm 56:8

CONTENTS

The material you will find here is realistic. It comes from years of counseling women and couples through the tragic results of sexual immorality, including adultery.

The couples I have written about for illustration purposes are fictitious; composites of many people I have counseled over the years and should not be misconstrued as being any specific persons, living or dead. I have aimed to keep the situations and reactions as realistic as possible for the greatest benefit to the reader.

ACKNOWLEDGEMENTS

I would like to thank all those who shared their hearts and heartaches with me—you know who you are! I cherish the relationships we have built along the way, and I pray the Lord would continue the wonderful work He has begun in each of your lives.

I would like to acknowledge the work of Pastor Bruce Roeder, my friend and co-laborer in Christ. The chapters on the Covenantal Relationship and the section on Eros Defiled were drawn from lessons he wrote for the counselor training program that we worked on together. Bruce, you continue to encourage me through your writings and I am thankful for the cooperative relationship we share with our materials from the good ol' days!

My friend and fellow biblical counselor Dr. Robert Kellemen has made a great impact on me and on my counseling methodology in the area of suffering. His fantastic book, *God's Healing for Life's Losses*, has been ever so helpful as I have navigated these waters in preparing for chapter 15 on suffering. He has graciously allowed me to use his intellectual property in this way, and for this I am extremely grateful.

I am thankful for the editing team: Sherrie Holman, Susan Verstraete, Emily Duffey, and Suzanne Holland who painstakingly edited each version of the manuscript. I am also grateful to my friend, Jody Lokken who puts it all together.

Thank you to my friends and church family—especially my small group people: Carol and John, Sandra and Don, Shelly and Brent and Emily who have prayed for me and listened to me as I struggled working through this book.

I would especially like to thank my husband Larry who is the only one on Earth who knows the cries of my soul. You are my always and forever love.

I also want to thank Amber Jennings for the cover design and layout of the book.

PREFACE

When Your Spouse Has Sexually Sinned

For many reading this book, it is too late. You have learned your husband/wife has been involved in some aspect of sexual immorality and you are reading this book looking for help, healing, and hope. You have no idea what to do with the heartache that has claimed your life. Others have not experienced the heartache of spousal betrayal, but may be wondering what to look for, or how you will know s/he is straying.

Sex is a wonderful gift from God. What's sad about writing this book is that I am attempting to undo damage already done in some respects.

You are most likely reading this because you have been touched by sexual immorality. You may have been involved sexually before you were married, either with your spouse or someone else. You or your spouse may have committed adultery. You may be someone's victim; you may have developed lust issues through pornography, romance novels, soap operas or an overactive thought life. Your spouse may currently be involved in sexual immorality, or maybe YOU are.

You might also be uncomfortable, wondering if you will be exposed or if what you are about to read will hit too close to home.

Unless you live in a cave, there are corruptions of sexuality that you and I as Christians are going to have to face. We live in a highly sexualized culture where women are often treated as objects of sexual gratification and children are sold for sexual pleasure. There appears to be little that is private and morality seems to have taken an extended holiday.

In my counseling office, I have seen the fallout from all kinds of sexual sin that has taken place in the workplace, and the church, between friends and neighbors, and sadly even among people I know and love.

You need to know this: sexual sin is pervasive and invasive. It does not care about your income, race, color or creed. Sexual sin is a captor and it takes hostages. You also need to know there is hope.

Because my ministry is primarily to God's people, this book is written for them. Rather than being generic in approach, I have aimed the counsel herein toward the hearts—the broken hearts—of those whose spouses have been sexually immoral. Some have been involved in watching pornography or participating in other lewd, voyeuristic behaviors such as going to strip clubs. Others have spouses who have committed adultery—physical adultery by having sexual contact with another man/woman or emotional adultery by being involved with another person without sexual contact.

No matter what kind of adultery your spouse has committed, when you learned of it your life was changed. Your world tilted off of its axis and you realized nothing would ever be the same again. This is true, nothing will be the same.

But it can be better.

Despite what your husband/wife has done, I want you to hear me clearly when I tell you that adultery does not have to ruin your life or your marriage. Adultery is a sinful act that was committed by your spouse. It does not define who you are.

INTRODUCTION

Historically, sexual issues have been considered a man's domain. It is critical that you understand that sexual immorality is not just for men any more. Women also struggle in growing numbers with many of the same issues men do, and for the very same reasons.

Why is it that people are not gripped by all sins to the same degree? What separates us? What makes one person what the world calls an addict, and the other a casual consumer? Science may have an answer one day, but to date there is nothing scientific that proves there is anything medical going on inside the body of an addict making them different from anyone else.

Many Christians involved in sexual immorality genuinely want to stop. They know it is wrong, and when they are not tempted, they *want* to stop. They are disgusted by their behaviors when they are able to think about them objectively.

I cannot and will not say that you as the spouse had no culpability whatsoever, because I don't know that. There are some marriages that are void of any sexual contact; the couple lives together, sleep together, and spend time together, but there is no sexual intimacy. This is a violation of 1 Corinthians 7 which clearly states that married couples are to engage in sexual intimacy for precisely this reason! Men and women were wired for sex in the confines of marriage.

Paul specifically says that we are not to withhold our bodies from our spouse. In fact, he says that when you marry, your body no longer belongs to you, but to your husband or wife. When sex is withheld in marriage it provides the occasion for sin in the thought life—wandering thoughts that lead to wandering hands and wandering bodies.

I would like to lay the blame squarely at the feet of Satan, but I cannot do that. Jeremiah 17:9 says that the heart is deceptive, and desperately wicked. The heart is so wicked, in fact, that we cannot and do not know the depths of the depravity that lives there; so wicked and so deceptive that we can rationalize our sinful desires and be lulled into thinking that our sin is justified because, "s/he would not . . . ," or because, "I don't feel . . . ," and, "God surely does not want me to live this way . . ."

I cannot say that you as the offended spouse have not been selfish, greedy, self-pitying, hateful or cruel to your husband/wife. You have to examine your life and ask God's help in examining your own heart to determine what sin you have contributed to taking the marriage to this point of brokenness.

Again, what your spouse did is not your fault; s/he is completely responsible for his/her own actions. You are responsible for yours. You must be willing to confess your sin to your spouse and ask his/her forgiveness for the sin that you have committed against him/her in the marriage.

You must determine to change the areas of your life that are problematic. These are not changes just to make you or your spouse happy, but changes that glorify God and further identify you as His child.

It is also possible that you have had a great marriage. Perhaps you and your spouse have had a great relationship that includes communication, companionship and an agreeable amount of sex that pleases both of you. Like any relationship, yours has had its ups and downs but overall you thought your marriage was impervious to this sort of thing. The revelation of sexual sin has completely blown you away.

You cannot comprehend the reality that your husband/wife has been involved in sexual sin. You did not see the signs; you did not see this coming. What you saw was a bright future ahead which you now realize was an oncoming train that ran you over.

You want to believe it was a mistake—a foolish and stupid mistake . . . a lapse in judgment or something done in a moment of thoughtlessness or drunkenness, something, *anything* other than what it truly is. You want to believe him/her when s/he says, "It meant nothing."

The hard thing to accept is that no matter what s/he says, they truly wanted this on some level, because sexual sin is a heart issue; it reveals the contents of the inner man. This is incredibly difficult to wrap your mind around and accept. It is sometimes even difficult for the offender to accept.

It is important that you realize sexual immorality does not happen in a vacuum and committing sexual sin is never an accident. A person cannot accidentally have sexual relations with another person; a car doesn't have auto pilot that drives the owner to the porn store or the strip club, or that cruises for prostitutes. There is always a decision to be made before typing XXX porn into the search bar on the computer, and then another decision to be made before clicking a link. To say that sexual sin is unintentional is a lie.

> We like to tell ourselves and our spouse that we didn't plan such a thing, that we never intended it to happen, or that it "just happened," as though we were sitting on a chair and were doused with water or something...

There is always some underlying heart issue that started long before s/he ever took the step of physical adultery or of clicking on that computer porn site. There is *always, always* thought, belief and desire that goes into making the decision to be immoral. It is not a decision that happens outside of the person. Nothing takes possession of an individual, forcing the body to operate independent of thoughts, beliefs or desires! It just does not happen.

Whatever compelled your husband or wife to commit sexual immorality was something s/he wanted and sought after. S/he was someplace s/he should not have been; your spouse was involved with someone in some way that s/he knew was wrong or dangerous to the marriage covenant.

There was time to think about where s/he was headed before the two of them got naked or performed sex acts with each other. There was time as they chatted online to close out the chat, delete the account, even unfriend on Facebook. There was time to get in the car, call his/her spouse, run away, sneak out the back, or be honest and say s/he could not do this, it could not go one step further.

The fact is . . . your husband/wife did not.

Because we are so adept at lying to ourselves, rationalizing and justifying our behavior, it is very easy to overlook this truth.

The human heart is set on gratifying self. This is a universal truth and it applies to everyone. Despite anything that has been said to you, what your spouse did was not your fault; it was their decision. What your husband/wife did was of his/her own volition.

S/he had a lust or desire of the heart that was not fulfilled. The lust or desire was most likely illegitimate, meaning it was not based in Scripture or was selfish and self-serving.

> *...being darkened in their understanding, excluded from the life of God because of them, because of the hardness of their heart; and they, having become callous, have given themselves over to sensuality for the practice of every kind of impurity with greediness.*
>
> Ephesians 4:18—19

You must understand that if it was not this sexual partner, it would have been someone else because your spouse has a sexual sin issue in his/her heart.

Those who have been regenerated by Christ and are fortunate to be in a good church are taught that they are to deny themselves, that life is not about them, and they are to live and use their lives to glorify God (Luke 9:23–24; Philippians 2:1; 1 Corinthians 10:31).

However, we are still sinners and often struggle with gargantuan desires of the flesh. Ephesians 4:18–19 says sinful desires make a person's heart hard to the truth of God's commands and can lead even a Christian to act as an unbeliever.

One man who committed physical adultery said he never imagined himself as the object of desire of another woman. His self-image led him to find it unbelievable that another woman besides his wife would find him attractive or desirable.

A woman who was adulterous had a comparable report. The man she was involved with paid her loving attention, complimented her, and told her she was beautiful.

Often men know they are the object of lustful looks by other women. Some were promiscuous before marriage and had other sexual partners right up to their wedding day. They enjoy the attention given to them by women and do not think there is anything wrong with flirting after marriage.

Many adulterers want to believe that they just fell into the relationship; they did nothing to promote it nor are they responsible for what happened.

Men and women who are caught using pornography will often give excuses for being found with it on their computers. They will say that they don't know how it got there, or they were surfing the internet for something innocent and something just popped up on their screen with no prompting from them. They may claim innocence saying they allowed a friend or their child to use the computer and this is how it appeared.

Sometimes a husband will admit he has been watching pornography and blame his wife for his need to do so. Men will say that their wives are not satisfying them sexually or often enough. Some will even try to legitimize their use of porn by saying their wives have a lack of interest in sex so they don't want to bother them with it. People give a variety of reasons for sexual immorality and adultery—too many to list, actually! Whatever the reason given you must understand there is really only *one* reason: they have a sinful heart.

Sorrow covers me like a blanket
It comes over me like a mist and covers me.

Sorrow is my constant companion.
Secrets live inside my heart and steal away a part of who I am.
Secrets that want and yearn to see the light of days
Secrets that when exposed will ruin the lives of many.

You were the love of my life, my Knight in Shining Armour
You rescued me and promised me your love was true.

I groan with anguish in my soul at the lies and betrayal.
I have been done a great wrong, an enormous wrong.
I would expect this from an enemy, not from the heart and soul of me.

I both shrink from you and cling to you.
I shrink from the horror you are and the dirty deed you have done me.
I despise the lies I now live
I am enraged at how your sin has affected me and will affect me for the rest of
my life.
I cling to you because I am afraid to be without you, oh soul of my soul, heart
of my heart, flesh of my flesh.

I pray the Lord will heal me
I pray He will restore me
I beg Him to protect me- from you..from her...from truth..from lies.

I trust the Lord and I fear He will show me more, more of things I do not think
I can bear.
I live in fear of the next revelation of truth
I watch you carefully, weighing your responses and reactions.

I do not trust you, but I am trying.
I do not believe you because you told me you would always be true...
I am tired of living a lie, and wondering if I am living a lie.

Your shame is so great that I fear that knowing what really went on would kill
me, and I fear the day I would learn it.

Save me oh Lord...save me, and restore to me a marriage that is whole and pure,
a man who is honest and true, and wholeness of mind and spirit.

—Anonymous

CHAPTER 1
The Covenantal Relationship

When we marry we make a covenant before God, with our spouse, to be faithful to the other. We are agreeing to bind and commit ourselves to our husband or wife for the rest of our earthly lives. God established this covenant when He brought Eve to Adam in the Garden and said they were "one flesh" (Genesis 2:24). In the marriage ceremony God is the one sealing the covenant. God takes the marriage covenant very seriously!

> *...Because the LORD has been a witness between you and the wife of your youth, against whom you have dealt treacherously, though she is your companion and your wife by covenant. But not one has done so who has a remnant of the Spirit. And what did that one do while he was seeking a godly offspring? Take heed then to your spirit, and let no one deal treacherously against the wife of your youth. "For I hate divorce," says the LORD, the God of Israel, "and him who covers his garment with wrong," says the LORD of hosts. "So take heed to your spirit, that you do not deal treacherously."*
> Malachi 2:14—16

To fully understand the ramifications of sexual immorality, we must first look at God's plan for marriage. Contrary to our current societal beliefs, marriage is not a contract. It is a covenant based on Genesis 2:18—25:

> *Then the LORD God said, "It is not good for the man to be alone; I will make him a helper suitable for him." Out of the ground the LORD God formed every beast of the field and every bird of the sky, and brought them to the man to see what he would call them; and whatever the man called a living creature, that was its name. The man gave names to all the cattle, and to the birds of the sky, and to every beast of the field, but for Adam there was not found a helper suitable for him. So the LORD God caused a deep sleep to fall upon the man, and he slept; then He took one of his ribs and closed up the flesh at that place. The*

LORD God fashioned into a woman the rib which He had taken from the man, and brought her to the man. The man said,

"This is now bone of my bones, and flesh of my flesh; She shall be called Woman, Because she was taken out of Man."

For this reason a man shall leave his father and his mother, and be joined to his wife; and they shall become one flesh. And the man and his wife were both naked and were not ashamed.
Genesis 2:18–25

A marriage covenant is a commitment a man and a woman make before God whereby they promise among other things, to be faithful to one another for the rest of their lives. God's expectation is that when you marry, it is forever. Marriage is a covenant before God; it is not a contract to be broken.

But from the beginning of creation, God made them male and female. "For this reason a man shall leave his father and mother, and the two shall become one flesh; so they are no longer two, but one flesh." What therefore God has joined together, let no man separate.
Mark 10:6–9

When you say those wedding vows you are committing to do these things: love, honor, respect, obey, submit, cherish, care for each other through good times and bad times, with and without money, when one of you is sick and, at some point in time, even while one of you is dying.

Wayne Mack, in his book *Strengthening Your Marriage*, says, "Marriage is a total commitment and a total sharing of the total person with another until death."[1]

This means that man and his wife share everything in life—their bodies, their possessions, their insights, their ideas, their abilities, their problems, their successes, their sufferings, and their failures.

Both husband and wife have to be as concerned with the needs of their spouse as they are with their own needs because they are no longer two individual people, but one flesh (Ephesians 5:22—33; Philippians 2:3—4; Matthew 22:39).

Becoming one flesh is much greater than the sexual union that takes place; it is the total givng of self to the other person. In a marriage where oneness exists, it should be hard to tell where one person begins and the other one ends.

Marriage vows make you companions for life and part of the obligation of the covenant is to meet each other's need for companionship. The expectation is that you like each other enough to want to spend time together, and that you have common interests and enjoy each other's company.

Marriage is an act of love where you vow to meet each other's needs for life. We all have legitimate needs and when we marry we expect that our spouse will love us and care for us and provide for us. We expect s/he will be our life-long mate and will be there when things go wrong or when we need help.

When you agree to marry someone you are committing yourself to do these things for the rest of your life. You are obligated to provide in a covenantal relationship.

A PRACTICAL AND PRACTICED COVENANT [2]
The Importance of a New and Better Covenant

Biblically speaking, covenants are either unconditional or conditional. The Old Covenant as a whole was conditional. God would either bless or curse Israel depending on if they kept or broke the Law of Stone. The covenant with Abraham was unconditional and God would keep the covenant (promises) regardless of what Abraham did or did not do.

> *"I do promise and covenant, before God and these witnesses, to be thy loving and faithful husband... I promise to love, honor, cherish, and protect you forsaking all others and holding only unto you as long as we both shall live."*
>
> -Traditional Marriage Vow

Christians are New Covenant believers that are more concerned with the Law of Christ (who is the fulfillment of the Old Covenant) than they are with a superficial adherence to the Law of Stone. Christians make an unconditional covenant with one another that is not based on the other's doing or not doing.

Let's see how this New Covenant might apply to a practical and practiced Covenant of Marriage.

> *For if that first covenant had been faultless, there would have been no occasion sought for a second. For finding fault with them, He says, "Behold, days are coming," says the Lord, "When I will effect a new covenant with the house of Israel and with the house of Judah; not like the covenant which I made with their fathers on the day when I took them by the hand to lead them out of the land of Egypt; for they did not continue in My covenant, and I did not care for them," says the Lord. "For this is the covenant that I will make with the house of Israel after those days," says the Lord: "I will put My laws into their minds, And I will write them on their hearts. And I will be their God, and they shall be My people. And they shall not teach everyone his fellow citizen, and everyone his brother, saying, 'Know the Lord,' for all will know Me, from the least to the greatest of them. For I will be merciful to their iniquities, and I will remember their sins no more."* Hebrews 8:7—12

> *Moreover, I will give you a new heart and put a new spirit within you; and I will remove the heart of stone from your flesh and give you a heart of flesh. I will put My Spirit within you and cause you to walk in My statutes, and you will be careful to observe My ordinances.* Ezekiel 36:26—27

Here is the point: The Old Covenant was primarily external. The New Covenant is *internal*. It's a change from the inside out. It's genuine heart change empowered by the Holy Spirit to seek to glorify God and serve others, especially husband and wife.

For the love of Christ compels us, because we judge thus: that if One died for all, then all died; and He died for all, that those who live should live no longer for themselves, but for Him who died for them and rose again.

2 Corinthians 5:14–15 (NKJV)

The conditional covenant is more like a contract. If you serve me, I'll serve you. If you don't serve me, I'll break the contract because you are not doing your part.

This differs from the New Covenant, where believers are motivated to serve one another because the love of Christ controls or *compels* them for the love of God is written on their hearts. They love God by loving their neighbor. Their closest neighbor is the person with whom they are making a covenant of marriage.

The one another acts of a covenant marriage are Christ-centered and reveal that Christ is operating in the person's heart regardless of how they may feel at any particular moment. The emotional eros type love that fuels the relationship at the outset gives way to the unconditional agape love that loves even when the other person does not deserve it.

When a man or woman takes the bait and consents to an adulterous relationship, they break the covenant they made with their spouse before God to be faithful and true to them, to keep themselves set apart only for the other, to honor them and cherish them. The adulterer breaks the vow to love.

Adultery is the antithesis of 1 Corinthians 13; is it not patient, kind or loving. Adultery is self-seeking, selfish, prideful and arrogant, and the exclusiveness of the relationship is blown away as s/he joins him/herself to another. Adultery destroys the oneness God intended in marriage.

CHAPTER 2
Sex: God Designed, Man Defiled

God Invented Sex

The biblical account of the first marriage is beautiful. We learn in Genesis 2:18—25 that God created Adam, the first man, to be different from everything else He created. Adam was the crowning glory of creation and was created in the image of God, according to His likeness (Genesis 1:26). Unlike the rest of what God made, Adam was given a soul and a will, and was capable of reason. He was also like God in that he was sinless and very good (Genesis 1:31).

As God caused all the other created things to pass before Adam to be named, Scripture says there was found no suitable helper for him (Genesis 2:20). There was no one else like Adam and God decreed in Genesis 2:18, "It is not good for the man to be alone; I will make him a helper suitable for him."

God created Eve to be Adam's perfect counterpart. She was created for him and to be like him, but different. His proclamation in Genesis 2:23 reveals his delight in God's handiwork!

There was no shame at their nakedness and there was no covering provided for their bodies. Their sexual love before the fall was pure, sweet and rapturous.

They reveled in each other's bodies and that is the way God intended it to be.

Let your fountain be blessed, and rejoice in the wife of your youth. As a loving hind and a graceful doe, let her breasts satisfy you at all times; be exhilarated always with her love. Proverbs 5:18—19

For this reason a man shall leave his father and his mother, and be joined to his wife; and they shall become one flesh. And the man and his wife were both naked and were not ashamed. -Genesis 2:24—25

We only need a few verses in Song of Solomon to understand what is being detailed for us is the intimate union of a man and woman.

> *Awake, O north wind, and come, wind of the south; make my garden breathe out fragrance, let its spices be wafted abroad. May my beloved come into his garden and eat its choice fruits.* Song of Solomon 4:16

In the New Testament we learn that the sexual union is intended to represent the intimate relationship between Jesus Christ and the church, between God and mankind (Mark 10:7—9; Matthew 19:6).

> *Husbands, love your wives, just as Christ also loved the church and gave Himself up for her, so that He might sanctify her, having cleansed her by the washing of water with the word, that He might present to Himself the church in all her glory, having no spot or wrinkle or any such thing; but that she would be holy and blameless. So husbands ought also to love their own wives as their own bodies. He who loves his own wife loves himself; for no one ever hated his own flesh, but nourishes and cherishes it, just as Christ also does the church, because we are members of His body. FOR THIS REASON A MAN SHALL LEAVE HIS FATHER AND MOTHER AND SHALL BE JOINED TO HIS WIFE, AND THE TWO SHALL BECOME ONE FLESH. This mystery is great; but I am speaking with reference to Christ and the church.* Ephesians 5:25—32

God repeatedly says the two are one flesh. Woven throughout the Scriptures is the message that marriage and the sexual union are to reflect the oneness God and man are to have in Christ. It is the most beautiful representation of the relationship Christ has with His Bride, the Church (Ephesians 5:31, 32).

This is one reason that Satan has made sex a primary target in Christian marriages. Anything he can do to spoil this most glorious and intimate picture is good for his purposes. Our enemy the devil has taken this beautiful picture, this one flesh relationship, and perverted it. His perversion of the sexual relationship is not accidental, it is intentional.

He chose the most accurate and intimate portrayal of Christ and the church and turned it into filth, smut and a mighty profitable business.

God's Intention for Sex

Married people are encouraged to participate in sex often and we are told in Scripture by God Himself that it is to be enjoyable (Proverbs 5:19). God was so determined to get that message across that He wrote an entire book of the Bible about it (Song of Solomon).

The sexual relationship is primarily for the creation of children (Genesis 1:28) and yet humans are created with the ability to enjoy these acts. In fact, God designed our bodies so well that our desire for the pleasure of sex is to be met by our spouses frequently to avoid sinning!

> *Nevertheless, because of sexual immorality, let each man have his own wife, and let each woman have her own husband. Let the husband render to his wife the affection due her, and likewise also the wife to her husband. The wife does not have authority over her own body, but the husband does. And likewise the husband does not have authority over his own body, but the wife does. Do not deprive one another except with consent for a time, that you may give yourselves to fasting and prayer; and come together again so that Satan does not tempt you because of your lack of self-control. But I say this as a concession, not as a commandment. For I wish that all men were even as I myself. But each one has his own gift from God, one in this manner and another in that.*
>
> 1 Corinthians 7:2—7 (NKJV)

The above passage teaches both husband and wife that they do not belong to themselves; they belong to one another. Belonging to one another in the physical sense means that sexual intimacy is to be for each other and with each other and no one else.

When each of them has their focus on gratifying the other the picture is beautiful and fulfilling. Contrary to what the entertainment industry promotes, the sexual union is others-oriented, not self-oriented. The ridiculous movie shots of men and women rolling around in the sheets are not intended to portray the attitude of selflessness in sexuality; they reflect the all about me mentality of the world. A godly husband is thoughtful and intentional about how to physically please his wife. Her gratification is a high priority for him because he is respecting her as much as he does himself. In Ephesians 5, husbands are told to love their wives as their own bodies. "After all, no one ever hated his own body," Paul writes, "but he feeds and cares for it, just as Christ does the church" (Ephesians 5:28, 29).

Likewise, a wife is to consider the gratification of her husband before her own. She is to put his pleasure and need first out of love and obedience. God did not design sex to be a chore or a duty to be done on a schedule or under duress; it is to be a loving expression of submission to the authority of God and the physical cravings of one's spouse.

This is an area where some women struggle. They recoil at the idea that anyone would own them, especially in this so-called enlightened age of feminism. The idea that a woman should have to submit her body to another person horrifies some women.

Women's heads have been filled with feministic lies that tell them that they can do as they please with their body ("my body, my choice") forgetting that they have been bought with a price (1 Corinthians 6:20) by the precious blood of Christ. The Christian woman does not have the biblical right to say she can do as she pleases with her body.

Men's heads have been filled with an attitude of entitlement. They place a high value on self-gratification because they have been taught wrongly about sexuality in marriage. Neither idea is correct for the couple who desires to honor God in the privacy of their intimate times.

The Fall of Sex
Eros is the name of the Greek god of **love**. The ancient Greeks distinguished four different kinds of love: *eros*, sexual love; *phileo*, to have affection for; *agapao*, to have regard for, be contented with; and *stergo*, used especially of the love of parents and children or a ruler and his subjects.[3]

The word erotic comes from the Greek word *eros,* which is the term for sexual love itself, as well as the god's name.[4]

Eros has been defiled and that is clear as we see how sex is used in our current culture in the context of love. This understanding of love is not what God intended sex to be for or about.

To understand how far we have come from a biblical understanding of eros we must return to the Garden of Eden.

Adam and Eve enjoyed each other physically and were sexually uninhibited. Even so, there was no perversion or any hint of immorality between them because there was no sin in them or in the world at that time. Their physical pleasure was pure and brought glory to God.

That all changed in one moment. In Genesis 3 we read the account of the fall of mankind. Satan is the Master of Deceit and he uses the same tricks and methods to bait the trap that he has employed since the Garden of Eden. Read the following narrative:

> *Now the serpent was the shrewdest of all the creatures the LORD God had made. "Really?" he asked the woman. "Did God really say you must not eat any of the fruit in the garden?"*

Satan planted doubt in the mind of the woman about what God had said.

> *"Of course we may eat it," the woman told him. "It's only the fruit from the tree at the center of the garden that we are not allowed to eat. God says we must not eat it or even touch it, or we will die."*

> *"You won't die!" the serpent hissed. "God knows that your eyes will be opened when you eat it. You will become just like God, knowing everything, both good and evil."*

The big lie occurs here, as well as the great temptation—"You will be like God." Man has wanted to be his own god since that time. We are deceived into believing that being our own god means the freedom to do whatever we want with no accountability.

Satan has not changed his tactics. In the area of sexual sin he tempts us with the same questions he used on Eve to cause us to doubt God and to encourage us to act as our own god.

Did God really say it is wrong to flirt with him/her? What will the harm be with just talking to him/her over the internet? It is not as though we are actually going to hook up or anything.

Did God actually restrict me from something pleasant? God knows my marriage is not good and He really wants me to be happy. Having sex with him/her makes me happy. I have a real peace about that in my heart.

Did he really deny me these pleasures? My body is made to respond sexually and I have no other means of release. Looking at pornography is not sinful; it is just the means to give me physical relief.

Is God really kind and good to deny me something? God made sex and He doesn't really care if I have sex or not, as long as no one is getting hurt.

The lies we choose to believe always promise great benefits.

> *The woman was convinced. The fruit looked so fresh and delicious, and it would make her so wise! So she ate some of the fruit. She also gave some to her husband, who was with her. Then he ate it, too. At that moment, their eyes were opened, and they suddenly felt shame at their nakedness. So they strung fig leaves together around their hips to cover themselves.*
> *Genesis 3:6—7 (NLT)*

Thus they succumbed to the lust of the eyes, the lust of the flesh, and the pride of life. Sin and guilt entered the world and the relationship between Adam and Eve changed forever.

And they heard the sound of the Lord God walking in the garden in the cool of the day, and the man and his wife hid themselves from the presence of the Lord God among the trees of the garden. But the Lord God called to the man and said to him, "Where are you?" And he said, "I heard the sound of you in the garden, and I was afraid, because I was naked, and I hid myself." He said, "Who told you that you were naked? Have you eaten of the tree of which I commanded you not to eat?" The man said, "The woman whom you gave to be with me, she gave me fruit of the tree, and I ate." Then the Lord God said to the woman, "What is this that you have done?" The woman said, "The serpent deceived me, and I ate."   Genesis 3:8—13 (ESV)

Notice what happened between Adam and Eve and God! They immediately knew fear. They understood that they were naked and exposed; they made coverings for themselves as they hid in the bushes, thinking God would not find them there.

When God confronted Adam and Eve and asked them a series of accountability questions they began to blame one another for their own actions. Adam blamed God for giving him Eve, he blamed Eve for making him eat of the tree, and the woman blamed the serpent.

There is no difference for people today who are involved in sexual immorality. Like Adam and Eve they believe that no one will know that they can cover their tracks and deceive their husband or wife. When they are discovered it is very common to shift the blame for the sinful behavior onto the spouse by citing unmet needs, feelings, and desires that have not been gratified.

In all areas of sexual sin, deceit is front and center.

Strong's defines deceit as *deceitful* and *deceitfulness*; In Scripture it means *fraud, falsehood, delusion* and even *idol.* Another source defines deceit as, "the act or practice of deceiving; concealment or distortion of the truth for the purpose of misleading; duplicity; fraud; cheating."[5]

CHAPTER 3
Biblical Examples of Sexual Sin

It has been said that there is nothing new under the sun. This is also true about sin; specifically, there is nothing new in the way of sexual sin under the sun. The record of mankind sinning sexually has been recorded since Genesis 4.

The Bible has much to say about sexual sin and its consequences. It gives us specific details about people who committed sexual sin. In some cases the personal consequences they bore are detailed, and in other cases the effects their sexual sin had on individuals and nations is explained.

Bigamy—

> *Lamech took to himself two wives: the name of the one was Adah, and the name of the other, Zillah.*
>
> Genesis 4:19

> *The Lord saw that the wickedness of man was great in the earth, and that every intention of the thoughts of his heart was only evil continually.*
>
> —Genesis 6:5 (ESV)

Bestiality—

> *If there is a man who lies with an animal, he shall surely be put to death; you shall also kill the animal. 'If there is a woman who approaches any animal to mate with it, you shall kill the woman and the animal; they shall surely be put to death. Their bloodguiltiness is upon them.*
>
> Leviticus 20:15—16

Sexual Surrogate—Sarai and Hagar—

> *Now Sarai, Abram's wife had borne him no children, and she had an Egyptian maid whose name was Hagar. So Sarai said to Abram, "Now behold, the LORD has prevented me from bearing children. Please go in to my maid; perhaps I will obtain children through her." And Abram listened to the voice of Sarai. After Abram had lived ten years in the land of Canaan, Abram's wife Sarai took Hagar the Egyptian, her maid, and gave her to*

her husband Abram as his wife. He went in to Hagar, and she
conceived . . . Genesis 16:1—4a

Homosexuality—Sodom and Gomorrah—
Before they lay down, the men of the city, the men of Sodom,
surrounded the house, both young and old, all the people
from every quarter; 5and they called to Lot and said to him,
"Where are the men who came to you tonight? Bring them out
to us that we may have relations with them."
Genesis 19:4—5

Sexual Trafficking—Lot and his daughters—
But Lot . . . said, "Please, my brothers, do not act wickedly.
Now behold, I have two daughters who have not had relations
with man; please let me bring them out to you, and do to them
whatever you like . . . " Genesis 19:6—8a

Prostitution—
None of the daughters of Israel shall be a cult prostitute, and
none of the sons of Israel shall be a cult prostitute. You shall
not bring the fee of a prostitute or the wages of a dog into the
house of the Lord your God in payment for any vow, for both of
these are an abomination to the Lord your God.
Deuteronomy 23:17—18, ESV

Incest—Lot and his daughters—
Lot went up from Zoar...and his two daughters with him...and he
stayed in a cave, he and his two daughters. Then the firstborn
said to the younger, "Our father is old, and there is not a man
on earth to come in to us after the manner of the earth. Come,
let us make our father drink wine, and let us lie with him that
we may preserve our family through our father." So they made
their father drink wine that night, and the firstborn went in and
lay with her father; and he did not know when she lay down or
when she arose. On the following day, the firstborn said to the
younger, "Behold, I lay last night with my father; let us make
him drink wine tonight also; then you go in and lie with him,
that we may preserve our family through our father." So they

made their father drink wine that night also, and the younger arose and lay with him; and he did not know when she lay down or when she arose. Thus both the daughters of Lot were with child by their father. The firstborn bore a son, and called his name Moab; he is the father of the Moabites to this day. As for the younger, she also bore a son, and called his name Ben-ammi; he is the father of the sons of Ammon to this day.

Genesis 19:30—38; see also 2 Samuel 13:1—15

Rape—

Now it was after this that Absalom the son of David had a beautiful sister whose name was Tamar, and Amnon the son of David loved her. Amnon was so frustrated because of his sister Tamar that he made himself ill, for she was a virgin, and it seemed hard to Amnon to do anything to her. But Amnon had a friend whose name was Jonadab, the son of Shimeah, David's brother; and Jonadab was a very shrewd man. He said to him, "O son of the king, why are you so depressed morning after morning? Will you not tell me?" Then Amnon said to him, "I am in love with Tamar, the sister of my brother Absalom." Jonadab then said to him, "Lie down on your bed and pretend to be ill; when your father comes to see you, say to him, 'Please let my sister Tamar come and give me some food to eat, and let her prepare the food in my sight, that I may see it and eat from her hand.'" So Amnon lay down and pretended to be ill; when the king came to see him, Amnon said to the king, "Please let my sister Tamar come and make me a couple of cakes in my sight, that I may eat from her hand."

Then David sent to the house for Tamar, saying, "Go now to your brother Amnon's house, and prepare food for him." So Tamar went to her brother Amnon's house, and he was lying down. And she took dough, kneaded it, made cakes in his sight, and baked the cakes. She took the pan and dished them out before him, but he refused to eat. And Amnon said, "Have everyone go out from me." So everyone went out from him. Then Amnon said to Tamar, "Bring the food into the bedroom, that I may eat from your hand." So Tamar took the cakes which she had made and brought them into the bedroom to her brother Amnon. When she brought them to him to eat, he took hold of her and said to her, "Come, lie with me, my sister." But she answered him, "No, my brother, do not violate me, for such a thing is not done in Israel; do not do this disgraceful thing! "As for me, where could I get rid of my reproach? And as for you, you will be like one of the fools in Israel. Now therefore, please speak to the king, for he will not withhold me from you." However, he would not listen to her; since he was stronger than she, he violated her and lay with her.

Then Amnon hated her with a very great hatred; for the hatred with which he hated her was greater than the love with which he had loved her.   2 Samuel 13:2—15

Adultery

King David—

David had at least eight wives and many concubines. His story includes adultery, murder, and polygamy—

1, 2 Samuel; 1 Chronicles 3:5

It happened, late one afternoon, when David arose from his couch and was walking on the roof of the king's house, that he saw from the roof a woman bathing; and the woman was very beautiful. And David sent and inquired about the woman. And one said, "Is not this Bathsheba, the daughter of Eliam, the wife of Uriah the Hittite?" So David sent messengers and took her, and she came to him, and he lay with her. (Now she had been purifying herself from her uncleanness.) Then she returned to her house. And the woman conceived, and she sent and told David, "I am pregnant."   2 Samuel 11:2—5 (ESV)

King Solomon—

Now King Solomon loved many foreign women along with the daughter of Pharaoh: Moabite, Ammonite, Edomite, Sidonian, and Hittite women, 2from the nations concerning which the LORD had said to the sons of Israel, "You shall not associate with them, nor shall they associate with you, for they will surely turn your heart away after their gods." Solomon held fast to these in love. He had seven hundred wives, princesses, and three hundred concubines, and his wives turned his heart away.   1 Kings 11:1—3

Under the Law, people found to be involved in sexual immorality paid a price. Usually, it cost them their life (Deuteronomy 22:22—29), but in some cases there was a cash or property payment due to the family of a young woman who had been violated. The man was also required to marry her. (Genesis 22:16—17)

Porneia

The word "pornography" comes from the Greek word *porneia*. As you look over the list below you will see that much of what society has deemed acceptable sexual behavior has its roots in this important Greek word.

Some of the behaviors that are included in porneia are:

Pedophilia—sex with children
Polygamy—multiple spouses
Bigamy—marrying one while married to another
Bestiality—sex with animals
Necrophilia—sex with the dead
Bondage and Domination—includes the consensual use of restraint, domination, and fantasy power role play
Homosexuality—sex with the same gender
Fornication—sex outside of marriage
Prostitution—sex for payment
Phone sex—a type of virtual sex that refers to sexually explicit conversation between one or more persons via telephone, especially when at least one of the participants masturbates or engages in sexual fantasy.[6]
Masturbation—sexual self-stimulation and self-gratification usually involving the use of pornography
Rape—forced sexual intercourse
Pornography—sexually explicit pictures, writing, or other material with the purpose to cause sexual arousal
"Gentleman's Clubs"—strip clubs that offer pole dancing, lap dancing

and sometimes prostitution
Voyeurism—watching others commit sexual acts

Masturbation

Masturbation is also known as self-gratification, self-stimulation, and self-sex.

According to one website, "The Bible does not specifically prohibit masturbation, or deliberate self-stimulation of the sexual organ to the point of orgasm … Masturbation is an act of self-gratification rather than a part of giving gratification and pleasure to one's partner."[7]

There are certainly direct commands to avoid types of sexual behavior such as adultery (Exodus 20:14), bestiality (Leviticus 18:23), homosexuality (1 Corinthians 6:9), fornication (Ephesians 5:3), orgies (Romans 13:13; Galatians 5:21) and the like, but nothing that *directly* tells a person not to participate in self-gratifying sexual conduct. However, there is nothing telling a person **to** do it, either.

I cannot say the Bible says something that it does not say. What is required is that we look further at what Scripture says about sexual immorality to determine if masturbation, despite not being specifically mentioned, it is included in some other aspect of that group of sins.

Most people who engage in this practice achieve a state of arousal by viewing or reading pornography, either hard-core or suggestive enough to bring arousal to the forefront of the mind. Because the mind is so effective at storing information, often a person can recall something that has been previously viewed or read to meditate on any time. If you want to engage in self-gratification you find this helpful; those who want to overcome this behavior find it a curse.

I think we all would agree that the consumption of pornography of any kind is sinful. It is certainly voyeurism and may even be adultery. Pornography both creates and feeds sinful lusts in the flesh, something Scripture commands us to abandon.

For you have spent enough time in the past doing what pagans choose to do—living in debauchery, lust, drunkenness, orgies, carousing and detestable idolatry.

1 Peter 4:3 (NIV)

Debauchery (extreme indulgence in immorality) will be the inevitable result of pornography. While many claim to be able to "moderate" with pornography, statistically people gravitate toward more and more forbidden behaviors as they view it. This in my opinion is one evidence that our flesh grows more corrupt (Ephesians 4:22) the more it is fed. Scripture is also clear on our obligation to put to death the desires of the flesh.

Put to death, therefore, whatever belongs to your earthly nature: sexual immorality (porneia—unlawful lust), *impurity* (physical or moral uncleanliness), *lust* (suffering a passionate lust), *evil desires* (a longing for forbidden desire) and *greed* (covetous practices), *which is idolatry.* Colossians 3:5 (NIV)

The question before us then, is this: is masturbation a form of sexual immorality? Based on the above Scripture, I would say it is. The bottom line is sexual self-stimulation stirs up an unlawful lust and leads to forbidden desires and passions that cannot be righteously satisfied.

Fornication

Fornication is any unlawful sex and is usually used to describe sex between two unmarried people. Biblically, fornication is included in the definition of porneia alongside adultery and homosexuality. Most people in our culture do not consider sex outside of marriage to be a problem, as long as both are consenting adults. The Bible says differently; it is called sin.

Those who are engaged, living together, sleeping together, in a committed monogamous relationship and are having sexual activity between them are all committing the sin of fornication.

Flee immorality. Every other sin that a man commits is outside the body, but the immoral man sins against his own body. Or do you not know that your body is a temple of the Holy Spirit who is in you, whom you have from God, and that you are not your own? For you have been bought with a price: therefore glorify God in your body.

1 Corinthians 6:18—20

I always knew it was wrong, but I let him talk me into it. I was raised in a Christian home and so was he. We had sex for months before our wedding, and I begged him to stop as a wedding present to me for the two weeks prior to our wedding. He reluctantly consented. Our wedding night was a disaster for me. I had no joy or anticipation for the event of our becoming husband and wife in the physical sense. It felt like there was nothing special about it at all. After he was asleep I went and cried in the bathroom for hours. I thought, 'Is this all there is now?' I dread sex now. I change in the bathroom or sneak to bed ahead of him because I don't want to give him any opportunity to become aroused or to have to tell him "no" again. He gets so mad at me when I tell him I am not in the mood, and it has begun to affect our marriage. I am so angry at him for making me have sex when I don't want to! He is selfish and is only thinking about himself. He says he needs it, and I don't believe him. I am fine without it, why can't he be?

~ Jenny

The body of a Christian belongs to God and is to be used for His purposes. There is no such thing as harmless fornication, no matter how the world tries to spin it to make it acceptable.

Emotional Adultery

With the advent of social networking sites people are now able to connect with friends around the globe. Like anything, these sites can be used for good and bad purposes. Social networking sites like Facebook and MySpace provide easy access to old flames, school friends, and former lovers.

It should be no surprise that we see skyrocketing divorce statistics (Facebook is now mentioned in 33% of divorce proceedings[8]) involving married people who find a long lost love and reconnect via a social networking site.

It is never wise for married people to "friend" people of the opposite sex. Those who have done this overwhelmingly regret it. Many of those who have fallen prey to a Facebook romance report that they never intended it to happen; they were just looking up an old friend.

Social networks provide shields of protection through privacy settings that deceive users into thinking it is safe to divulge information about their lives that is better kept private. Users believe that geographical distance will prevent them from actually making a physical connection with their "friend" and that reminiscing about days gone by is harmless. It *seems* harmless to flirt a little with an old boyfriend or girlfriend but it is not. If s/he was someone you were interested in before, what makes you think you won't be interested again?

An on-line relationship is not multi-dimensional; it is limited to the written word and selected pictures of a person. It is idealistic in that the people on either end of the connection reveal only what they want to have seen about themselves. This makes it easy to develop a strong emotional attachment to the other person and to "fall in love" with him or her. As that emotional connection develops, the husband/wife begins to be edited out as the "friend" becomes the new confidant.

An emotional affair can be as devastating to a marriage as a physical affair. When a husband/wife develops an on line relationship they *are* developing a *relationship* no matter how dimensionally restricted it is. There is sharing of daily life and the emotions, thoughts, beliefs, desires and feelings that accompany it.

I reconnected with an old high school friend on Facebook. It seemed so innocent at the time! We spent time on "chat" catching up about our lives over the years since graduation.

Before long she began to share information of a more personal nature with me and I found my feelings becoming involved. When she asked me to keep our conversations private and not inform my wife I hesitantly agreed to her request.

Over the days and weeks we emailed and chatted and sent private messages back and forth. We went so far as to create fake emails and false Facebook profiles to keep our relationship secret. We shared all the events of daily life with each other and I shared things, personal and private things, about my wife and marriage.

Looking back on it now, I see that over time I noticed these details appearing in our conversations, and she always subtly painted my wife and marriage in a negative light. Seeds of dissatisfaction began to grow inside of me as I considered what she said, and soon I started to see my wife as lacking the qualities I found in the other woman.

I found myself "in love" with her.

~Victor

Physical Adultery

Physical adultery takes place when a married person has sexual relations with someone other than his/her spouse. This may be the most damaging form of sexual sin. It shatters the one-flesh relationship, trust, intimacy and unity of marriage and can ruin the lives of everyone involved with both people who committed the sin.

It is perhaps difficult to comprehend that Christians commit adultery. People who attend church every Sunday are as susceptible to the lusts of the flesh as their non-Christian counterparts. We struggle to understand how this can happen, how a Christian who attends church, reads their Bible, and professes a love for God can fall into such deep sin, but it happens with shocking regularity.

> I remember driving back home after what I had done. It was the darkest part of the night right before the dawn which was fitting for my mindset at that time. I clearly recall passing the airport and thinking about what had just happened. My soul was enveloped in blackness and I thought to myself, "Well, I have really done it now. I have broken one of the Commandments and I am surely going to hell." Little did I know, I was already at its gate.
>
> *~Anna*

CHAPTER 4
The Scourge of Pornography

Pornography

Pornography is the selling of sexually explicit pictures, writing, or other material whose purpose is to cause sexual arousal. It is motionless or moving images, usually of women but more often of teenagers and children in varying states of nudity, posing or performing erotic acts with men, women, animals, machines or other props.

We have long known that pornography is a problem for many men. It used to be in a brown wrapper behind the counter. A man had to be willing to ask for it. Next, it went to home delivery in a brown wrapper, and now it is at the check-out counter at the store titled as popular women's magazines.

"Dirty movies" used to be shown in run down theaters on the wrong side of town. Now, standalone stores with benign and deceptive names sell pornographic movies, and people walk into them in broad daylight—without shame.

Additionally, the internet has brought all kinds of pornography into the home. You can view or read anything you want from your living room without a subscription. A person can download a torrent, share a file, or use a friend's thumb drive to view a porn flick.

The Scourge of Pornography[9]

Pornography movies—13.3 Billion in U.S.
U.S. porn revenue exceeds all combined revenues of ABC, CBS, and NBC—over 6 billion
Porn websites—4.2 million (12% of total websites)
Monthly porn downloads—1.5 billion (35% of all downloads)
8-16—The age of children having viewed porn online—90% (most while doing homework)

Pornography is not just for men anymore either. A flood of new viewers have latched on to the porn bandwagon—and that group is women. Young and old, Christian and non-Christian, women are viewing pornography in record numbers.

My husband and I used to watch pornography together throughout our many years of marriage, even continuing the practice after we were saved. We discontinued this after our pastor told us it was wrong.

My husband and I really enjoyed watching the movies together and we did not think there was anything wrong with it as long as we were only actually having sex with each other.

It has been a number of years now, and I have to say that our sexual life is not fulfilling for me. I would classify myself as someone who is rarely interested in sex.

One night I was sleepless and put on the T.V. I found and extended pornographic infomercial. I wanted to change the channel but I didn't want to at the same time. I knew this was bad, but I was pulled in so fast!

I knew I had fallen, and I knew it as I was doing it! I knew as I was becoming aroused and touching myself that I was headed into dangerous waters. I ignored and nearly physically pushed the warnings of the Holy Spirit away from me.

I remember talking to God telling him I knew what I was about to do was wrong but I was too far gone. He should look the other way. I had to find release.

Afterward, I wanted to keep my eyes down. I did not want to look up because I did not want to meet the eyes of God. I was filled with an empty hollow sensation. I waited for the condemnation to come, the feelings of sneering condemnation. They never did. What came instead was something like a gentle voice saying, 'Well, did you find what you were looking for in that? Was it satisfying? Was it worth it to you?' I had do admit it was not. The Lord reminded me that what I was engaged in was a sham and an empty representation of what the sexual union with my husband was.

Despite that, I quickly returned to seeking out porn on the internew. I am once again trapped and don't know how to stop it anymore.

~Violet

There are a growing number of women like "Violet" in our churches.

I grew up hearing that that women don't enjoy looking at naked bodies the way men do, and it is true that most women are stimulated more by mind and imagination than by visuals. Yet women are being seduced into the world of pornography.

Some couples view it together as foreplay. Others use it to spice up their sex lives when things get boring after a number of years. The rationalization they use is that this practice is acceptable because they are married and actually having sex with each other. However, from a biblical perspective this behavior is still sinful! Pornography perverts what God intends for the sexual relationship in marriage.

Pornography and women is a relatively new phenomenon. Until recently, it was not widely known that women also enjoy looking at porn; a female "porn addict" is no longer considered rare. The woman who looks at pornography often places herself in the role of the women in the pictures or movies, being daring, uninhibited, and bold. It enables the socially and sexually conservative woman to act out her fantasies and do things she would never dare dream of doing in real life.

Women and Pornography[10]

- 9.4 million women access adult web sites each month
- 17% of all women struggle with porn addiction
- 70% of women keep porn viewing a secret
- 1 in 3 visitors to all adult web sites are women

Statistics[9] say that women who view porn are more likely to act out the behaviors they see in pornographic movies such as having multiple partners, casual sex, or extra-marital affairs.

Porn does not have to be hard core or an internet download—you can find it on your television every day in the form of reality television. Cable channels are replete with programs featuring men and women involved in various aspects of pornography.

Daytime network television used to play many soap operas for women who stayed at home and raised children. Over the last 20 years soap operas became soft core pornography with serial adultery, fornication, and sexual themes being prominent. Many women were so hooked into them that they would record the daily episodes while they were at work to watch over the weekend. The majority of "soaps" have faded in the ratings and many have been canceled in the past couple of years.

There are also cable stations that are geared for women, like Lifetime and WE that feature soft core pornography.

Our teenage sons and daughters see copious amounts of pornographic material if they are watching MTV, VH1, or any of those reality shows featuring a group of men or women trying to win a person as a prize.

Women often fail to understand that if they are reading romance novels, they are reading soft core pornography intended to cause sexual arousal. As you might guess, masturbation almost always accompanies viewing of illicit sexual material of any kind.

Why View Pornography

> *Hell and Destruction are never full; so the eyes of man are never satisfied.*　　　　　　　　　　　Proverbs 27:20 (NKJV)

After wading through hundreds of pages of internet articles and reading dozens and dozens of media, what I have learned is that married men say they view pornography because they can live out sexual fantasies, have a variety of sexual partners without hurting anyone and relieve the boredom of routine sex with their wives.

Most married women say they view pornography in order to live out sexual fantasies, to spice up their sex lives, get ideas for sex, and prepare for sex with their husbands. Some married women say they view pornography because they do not achieve sexual satisfaction with intercourse.

When a woman learns that her husband has been viewing pornography, she may be understandably angry, upset, hurt, and have feelings of betrayal. She may accuse her husband of committing adultery and tell him she wants a divorce. Her number one goal is to get him to stop.

Often, through many tears, she tries to explain to him how much he has hurt her by viewing porn. She will cite her fears that she is not attractive enough or woman enough for him and blame herself for failure to please him. She may beg him to stop, plead with him, and sometimes offer to view it with him in hopes of shocking him into stopping. She might use other forms of manipulation including ranting, tantruming, degrading and humiliating him, threatening exposure and/or divorce.

Other women will capitulate to the desires of their husband and passively allow him to view it, and some will be drawn into the pornographic world by their husband.

When a man learns his wife has been viewing pornography he may also be hurt and angry. However, he might also be very glad she is interested in pornography. A husband is more likely to ask his wife what he can do to help change things to make sex better for her. Fewer men than women think of viewing pornography as being adulterous.

The discovery of the use of pornography by a spouse can bring feelings of inadequacy to both husband and wife. The thought, "I can't compete with that" is prevalent and both sexes cite a feeling of failure to meet their spouse's needs.

The excuses offered the most as reasons by the spouse who views pornography are discounted as invalid when presented to a random sampling of husbands and wives.[11]

Both spouses said that if their husband/wife would have communicated their sexual needs, that in most instances they would have been willing to meet those needs (so long as the requests were not considered deviant).

There are studies that seem to support the theories that pornography use changes how a person thinks and responds to sexual stimuli; I read a number of these studies in preparing for this section of the book. Survey responses also support the idea that the desire for harder core pornography increases the more someone watches it. While I do place some value on the studies, their current conclusions only support what God has communicated through the Bible.

Heart Issues in Pornography Lovers

> *They count it a pleasure to revel in the daytime. They are stains and blemishes, reveling in their deceptions, as they carouse with you, having eyes full of adultery that never cease from sin, enticing unstable souls, having a heart trained in greed, accursed children; forsaking the right way, they have gone astray...*   2 Peter 2:13a—15a

A heart that is trained in greed is a heart that is focused on self. As in all other forms of sinfulness, people who view pornography have their thoughts, beliefs, and desires set on fulfilling the lust of the flesh and feeding the desires of the heart.

Idolatry, pride, greed, selfishness, and rebellion are just a few of the major issues of the heart that one must recognize and admit in order to break free.

The focus when viewing pornography is on meeting the felt needs of the moment. The thoughts are focused on "self" and viewers truly believe they *have* to fulfill the desires that they have in the moments of temptation. This is why viewing porn is idolatrous! Their heart is filled with pride as they think that meeting their perceived needs and feelings are all that matters.

The feelings and desires a person has from the sexual stimulation from pornography begin to demand allegiance and come to rule the user. Regardless of how little a person intends to view it, in relatively short order pornography reveals itself as something that cannot be set aside. The pleasurable feelings and physical release a person derives from it become a ruling force in life. Additionally, the original stimulating features of basic pornography become mundane and the lusty desires head toward harder and harder pornographic features. This is why greed is closely related to idolatry! What satisfied a man or woman last week will not be enough in a month. The flesh is never satisfied.

Lust-driven individuals are rarely rational thinkers in the moment. All that can be thought about is sating those desires without discovery. There are no thoughts of others, marriage vows, or spiritual consequences while watching XXX porn. Frequently, the only thoughts of their spouse are often about how they don't ever want them to find out and potentially take this avenue of self-gratification away.

The thoughts of entitlement come from the heart. The porn user believes that they have a "right" to feel good sexually and to gratify sexual "needs." It quickly becomes a major stronghold of idolatry in a person's life and because the pleasure senses are deeply affected by pornography, telling someone to "stop it" will fall far short of accomplishing the goal. This is the reason that commanding a spouse to cease their pornography habit is rarely effectual.

Heart Issues of Pornography

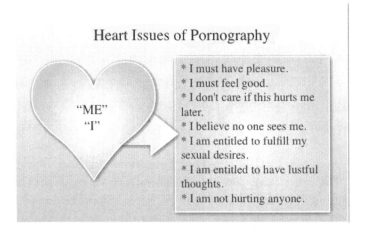

"ME"
"I"

* I must have pleasure.
* I must feel good.
* I don't care if this hurts me later.
* I believe no one sees me.
* I am entitled to fulfill my sexual desires.
* I am entitled to have lustful thoughts.
* I am not hurting anyone.

Pornography users are prideful people because they become their own god, determining biblical standards don't apply to them, and that they can make their own rules. Often the rules are centered on their belief that as long as no one knows they view pornography, no one gets hurt. It is perceived as a victimless habit which is untrue.

My Spouse Views Porn, What Do I Do Now?

Because pornography is at its base a heart issue, the person who views it must seek treatment at that level. There are many wonderful books and programs to help someone who is hooked on porn[12] get free from its domination. Any help a person receives on sexual sin must be more than "stop that." The counseling must be primarily about repentance and change to glorify God. It is my hope that your loved one has started that process already.

What about you? What are you to do now that you know your spouse has struggles with pornography? There are some practical things that can be done to decrease the access s/he has to pornography such as blocks on the computers and canceling internet/cable television. A person can also be placed on a time monitoring system, meaning all time away from you must be accounted for. This would be helpful if your spouse had a habit of frequenting adult entertainment stores.

While these things are helpful and are what we consider to be measures of accountability, you must remember that you cannot stop your spouse from sinning. You can set up every safeguard and system known to mankind but if s/he wants to return to that cesspool, they will. That is the first thing you must accept.

Acceptance of sexual sin is hard, hurtful, and might seem impossible. Typically, the husbands and wives who learn that their spouse is involved with pornography have many questions. They want to know why s/he had to look at that stuff. They want to know why they were not enough to sexually satisfy their spouse, how s/he could be so perverted, and there is the question that is asked in the deepest part of the heart of the wounded spouse: what is wrong with me?

The wounded spouse is left confused and insecure. A godly man whose wife is lusting after what she sees in pornography wonders why he does not meet her sexual needs. He may struggle with the knowledge that his wife wants to view such things and the knowledge that she masturbates while watching it is a deep wound to his masculinity.

A less than godly man can be sexually aroused by the knowledge that his wife is interested in viewing it with him. Until recently, it has been assumed that women were not turned on by viewing pornographic movies. The ability to watch a video stream and read erotica on the computer with little interruption during the day seems to have changed the minds of many women who previously found it disgusting.

Some men think that viewing it together would be a good thing or that it is a great way to spice up their sex life. This does not help either person to repent.

It seems that when a woman learns her husband is viewing pornography the impact is much greater. What women have told me time and time again is they are devastated by this revelation. There is no way to compete with the surgically altered and silicone injected bodies in those movies and magazines, and there is no way most Christian women would consent to some of the activities in the movies either.

They discover their husband has an appetite for things they are unwilling or unable to provide. Women have told me they are humiliated by the knowledge that their husband has sought out pornography. The revelation adds insecurity, fear and shame to what most women already see as lacking in themselves physically and sexually.

What I want you to know is that if your husband or wife is viewing pornography, it is not your fault. You did not do or say anything that would "make" them view or read it. As I said previously, this is a desire of the flesh that s/he is choosing to gratify.

Living with the Porn Addicted Spouse
I have been asked many times if viewing pornography qualifies as adultery and gives a spouse the biblical "right" to seek a divorce.

Because I address the issue of divorce and sexual sin elsewhere in this book I shall not go into that here.

The thoughts about pornography as "adultery" vary from person to person and church to church. Some believers are staunch in their opinion that looking at pornography and/or masturbating are adulterous because the viewer is "having sex" with another man or woman in their mind and being physically gratified while watching it. It is a "pretend affair" with a man or woman on the screen.

Other people believe that if it is not "hurting anyone" or the spouse does not have a problem with it then it is not a problem. They would rather their husband/wife view pornography than seek out a prostitute or "have an affair."

I believe it is what the Bible says about all kinds of sexual sin that matters.

Jesus said:

> *You have heard that it was said, 'YOU SHALL NOT COMMIT ADULTERY'; but I say to you that everyone who looks at a woman with lust for her has already committed adultery with her in his heart. If your right eye makes you stumble, tear it out and throw it from you; for it is better for you to lose one of the parts of your body, than for your whole body to be thrown into hell. If your right hand makes you stumble, cut it off and throw it from you; for it is better for you to lose one of the parts of your body, than for your whole body to go into hell.*
> Matthew 5:27—30

To the sex addict Jesus says, "Lust is the problem." He says it is a large enough problem to consider amputating the part of your body that will not submit to obedience. Of course, I am not promoting self-mutilation of the physical body, but I am suggesting that a person must take the biblical attitude of the heart so seriously that if amputation or plucking out an eye was the prescribed solution to eliminating the sin of lust from your life you would do it.

There is a desperation in such thinking, isn't there? It is the sort of desperation that claws and fights to get away from something or someone who will kill them or cause them great bodily harm. Sadly, most people who lust after the thrills of pornography do not understand that they are being led straight into destruction. They are indeed experiencing great bodily harm and more than that, they are experiencing destruction of the heart and soul. They are redirecting the pathways in their brain and exposing the pleasure sensors in their brain to stimuli that cannot be replicated in real life. They are destroying themselves from the inside out just as Scripture tells us will happen when a person indulges in sin[13] (Proverbs 6:26).

Sexual sin is **sin**—period. It is not a "mistake" or a "problem." To use that sort of terminology reduces the seriousness of the sinful pattern of life that has developed. It is sin, so I urge you not to minimize it when you speak of it just because it may evoke uncomfortable feelings. There **should** be discomfort because immorality is wrong and when a Christian is exposed to sin there should be discomfort involved!

As his/her spouse, you must understand that overcoming this sinful issue will not be easy for your spouse because sexuality is everywhere in one form or another. Every other billboard, commercial, magazine cover, or television program contains ungodly aspects of sex in our current era. This makes it incredibly difficult for a person striving to overcome sinful sexual thoughts, beliefs, and desires for "normal" sexuality to achieve it while living in the world.

You cannot badger him/her to stop lusting for it, and all the threats and manipulations in the world will not change his/her heart. The road back to sanity may be short or very, very long depending on the length of time your spouse has been viewing pornography and how graphic and explicit the pornography has to be for his/her lust to be sated.

You have to give up the idea that you can control him/her or control the outcome because you cannot. It is a very helpless feeling and can lead to despair and sorrow without hope if you see him/her fail again and again.

You must understand that if your spouse is looking at porn it is not your fault and you are not responsible. You did not fail him/her in any way. Your husband/wife went looking for something to satisfy lusts and desires of the flesh that *are not legitimate*. Your spouse has no right before God or you to desire these things.

As I said previously, you must pray for your spouse to repent but you have no control if s/he does. Do not condone any ongoing sexual sin in your husband/wife. Allow the involvement of the church leadership to go forward if your spouse is a Christian and has involvement in the church. I am aware of several cases in which people have repented and returned to the church for restoration after being turned over to the world (1 Corinthians 5:4–5) for the destruction of the flesh.

Practical Suggestions
If your spouse is involved with internet pornography, install blocks on all the computers they can access. Many employers now have filters that will not allow pornography to be viewed on work computers or electronic devices. I wish I could say it was for purposes of morality, but it is more for the concerns about liability, primarily with kiddy porn; secondly, productivity increases when employees don't have access to porn on the job. In any case, it is helpful when a company blocks access to pornography on a work computer or device.

If possible, get rid of cable and the internet to eliminate access in the home.

Suggest a program such as *Setting Captives Free* which is available online and off line in workbook format. Pray for a strong accountability person to come into your spouse's life who will be able to speak truth and righteousness firmly to his/her heart.

Enlist the help of your church (if your spouse is a Christian) by suggesting an appointment with the Pastor or Biblical Counselor[14] in your church or area.

Talk openly, honestly, and above all, biblically with your husband/wife about the sin of sexual immorality. Venting your feelings to him/her will not be as helpful as speaking biblical truth will be. If hurt feelings and anger were enough to help a person change then there would be no two-time offenders in this area! Your words, feelings, hurt, anger, or rage is not enough to affect his/her heart, only the Word of God can do that.

> *For the Word of God is living and active and sharper than any two-edged sword, and piercing as far as the division of soul and spirit, of both joints and marrow, and able to judge the thoughts and intentions of the heart.*
>
> Hebrews 4:12

There are no more powerful words than those of the Living God. Immerse yourself in them, meditate on them, and memorize them so that you will always have a good word to speak.

> *Preach the word; be ready in season and out of season; reprove, rebuke, exhort, with great patience and instruction.*
>
> 2 Timothy 4:2

We have looked at the types of sexual sin most often committed; now let us turn our attention to the reasons why Christians commit sexual sin.

CHAPTER 5
Understanding the Heart

In popular culture, the heart is almost exclusively linked to emotions. If you have heard someone say, "Speak from the heart," they wanted you to say something about how you feel. If you have been told to "follow your heart" you were being told to follow your feelings. We live in a culture that is dominated by emotions or feelings.

"Feelings" have become the dominion of the secular therapeutic world. People go to counseling because they "feel bad" or "feel sad" or "feel anxious." They seek a psychiatrist, psychologist, or therapist because their emotions are out of balance and their moods are destabilized.

The Bible teaches us that God is not impressed with human wisdom about people and their problems. Contrary to humanistic thinking, we believe that God is actively involved in the lives of His creation. We know from Scripture that many of the problems that people face every day are specifically mentioned in the Bible, and that many other problems are inferred throughout the text.

> *The human heart has so many crannies where vanity hides, so many holes where falsehood lurks, is so decked out with deceiving hypocrisy, that it often dupes itself.*
>
> —John Calvin

His Word reveals to us why it is pure foolishness to look to man's wisdom for the solutions to the spiritual problems we face.

> *"For my thoughts are not your thoughts, neither are your ways my ways," declares the LORD. "As the heavens are higher than the earth, so are my ways higher than your ways and my thoughts than your thoughts."*
>
> Isaiah 55:8—9 (NIV)

This is why, in dealing with the people who have committed sexual sin, we cannot look to a secular source for help or wisdom; we must instead look to our Wonderful Counselor (Isaiah 9:6).

Christ was loving, truthful, honest, confrontational, discerning, wise, and a host of other things. In the counsel of Christ, we see that He did not excuse sin; He called people to repentance, and He expected change in the hearts and lives of those who heard the truth.

He will minister to both the perpetrator and the victim of sexual sin because He understands the emotional component of a person and how emotions can sway their actions. He challenges them not to live by their feelings, but to live in obedience to His commands. He gives the Christian the Person of the Holy Spirit to enable them to do that.

During His earthly ministry, Jesus ministered to the whole person. He healed their physical ailments and often used such to point to their spiritual sickness or their spiritual needs. Today, He continues His ministry to both the material man and the immaterial man as both aspects are involved in committing sexual sin.

Material and Immaterial Man
The Bible makes a distinction between immaterial and material man.

Immaterial Man	Material Man
Inner Man	Outer Man
Heart of man—Mind, will, emotions, spirit, soul, thoughts, beliefs, desires, feelings, affections, conscience, etc.	Body of man—Flesh, bones, organs, blood, muscles, etc.
Spiritually dead—Ephesians 2:1-3 or Spiritually alive—Ephesians 2:4-10	Physically dead or Physically alive
Can be spiritually dead yet physically alive	
Subject to corruption and moral breakdown Ephesians 4, Romans 1	Subject to decay and organic breakdown 2 Corinthians 4:16
Originator	Responder

No one denies that these two "parts" of us, interact with each other constantly. The inner man is the place of thought and reason (Matthew 13:15). It is also the place of feelings or affections (Ecclesiastes 7:9,

Isaiah 35:4). The will also resides there and the will is what enables us to make choices and decisions.

The Bible says that whatever is spiritual proceeds from the heart (Proverbs 23:7a) and the heart is the battleground for the mind, will, and emotions. A person's spiritual condition will determine what he does with his thoughts, emotions, perceptions and behaviors. We cannot separate physical actions and attitudes from the spiritual aspects of a person; they are linked by what Scripture defines as the heart.

"Heart, in the Bible, does not mean emotions or feelings, as it does today in Western society. Rather, it encompasses <u>everything</u> that goes on inside a person...

the heart is the mind, soul, or spirit thought of as opposed to what one sees and hears (the outer person). In other words, the whole of the inner person." Dr. Jay Adams[15]

The world defines heart as feelings. Thayer's Greek Dictionary defines heart (the Greek word *kardia*) as "the soul or mind, as it is the fountain and seat of the thoughts, passions, desires, appetites, affections, purposes, endeavors; of the will and character; of the soul so far as it is affected and stirred in a bad way or good, or of the soul as the seat of the sensibilities, affections, emotions, desires, appetites, passions."[16]

From these considerations, we can see that from a biblical perspective the heart and soul are one and the same thing, and by no means is the word "heart" confined to mean, "How we feel."

Tragedy results when people trust their feelings in order to make decisions or to "speak truth" to themselves. How many people have made life-altering decisions based on the fuzziness of the advice to "follow your heart?"

In my counseling office, I have had people tell me they have made a decision to divorce their spouse because they prayed about it and "had a peace in their heart." I am told, "God does not want me to be unhappy . . ." which props up their unspoken rationalization that their sinful actions are justified.

This kind of thinking is the Christian version of following your heart. The language reflects a subjective, experiential, feelings approach to life rather than a solid, scriptural approach.

The True Condition of the Heart

The "heart" is not truthful.

Many life changing and life wrecking decisions are made on the basis of "following your heart." You must realize that your heart lies to you all the time! If this were not the case, then how could people break up their marriages on the basis of feeling that their heart was telling them to do so?

We must realize how deceptive it is to trust our emotions. In our culture it is popular to say "trust you heart" but it really means to trust your emotions. We must begin to change our thinking—to think in a faith based manner rather than a "feeling based manner."

> *The heart is deceitful above all things, and desperately wicked;*
> *who can know it?* Jeremiah 17:9 (NKJV)

The prophet Jeremiah declares the heart is deceitful above all things and desperately wicked. At the *very least*, it means our hearts cannot be trusted. Yet, in our culture, we constantly hear that we are to follow our hearts, make the right heart choice, and we are told our hearts can be trusted to guide us. When these things are said, they are in fact, equating feelings with the heart.

Clearly, that notion is contradicted directly by what God says—do not trust your heart emotions because they are deceitful and cannot be trusted to lead you.

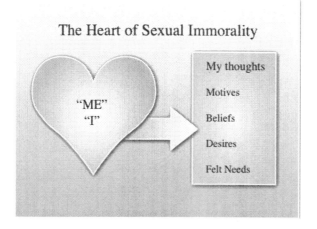

The Heart of Sexual Immorality

"ME" "I"

My thoughts

Motives

Beliefs

Desires

Felt Needs

Jesus Himself reveals the true condition of men's hearts.

> *For from within, out of the heart of men, proceed the evil thoughts, fornications, thefts, murders, adulteries . . .*
>
> Mark 7:21

The inner man is not "basically good," but seriously flawed and utterly corrupt. Without the grace of God, it will remain so. Since Adam, all men and women are sinners by nature and by choice, so it would be accurate to describe ourselves as basically depraved and not basically good (See Romans 3:9—18, 23; 5:10—12). Proverbs indicates it is folly to trust in one's own heart:

> *He who trusts in his own heart is a fool, but he who walks wisely will be delivered.*
>
> Proverbs 28:26

Instead, we are to trust in the Lord (and His Word) and not rely on our hearts.

> *Trust in the Lord with all your heart, and lean not on your own understanding.*
>
> Proverbs 3:5

Every aspect of our being is, by some extent, perverted by the sinfulness and wickedness that lurks within us. ***Knowing this, how could anyone advise another to follow his or her own heart?***

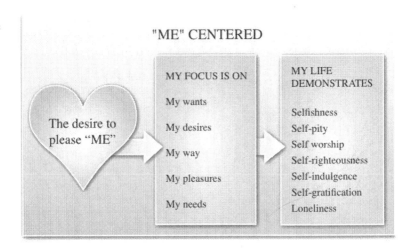

The diagram above shows how the desires of the sinful heart motivate the actions of real life.

What this diagram shows us is the out-flowing of the desires of the sinful heart into the actions of real life.

This is the reality: the deceitful heart is bent on satisfying *me*, having *my* own way, living life for *my* pleasures, with *me* at the center of *my* universe.

This leads a person to focus on their wants, desires, pleasures, and perceived needs. They become determined to have their own way.

When a person focuses on "self" and fulfilling the desires of their own heart, their life will demonstrate actions that glorify "self" and are focused only on pleasing themselves.

The Heart Reveals the Man

> *As in water, face reflects face, so a man's heart reveals the man.* Proverbs 27:19 (NKJV)

What does this Proverb mean? As water acts like a mirror and shows what we look like on the outside, the heart reflects and reveals what we are like on the inside.

64

But the things that proceed out of the mouth come from the heart,
and those defile the man. For out of the heart come evil thoughts,
murders, adulteries, fornications, thefts, false witness, slanders.
These are the things that defile the man . . .

Matthew 15:18—20a

If we are honest with ourselves, we may see that we have some of the
sin habits found in the above passage. If we are honest with ourselves,
we will begin to realize we tend to minimize our sinful heart attitudes.
As we read Jesus' words, we see our biggest problem lies within our
own hearts. Every action began as a thought; the thought was fueled by
a desire or belief; the desire or belief originated in the heart.

Jesus took the opportunity to speak to the attitudes of the heart when
He was questioned by the Pharisees and His disciples about pure foods
and ceremonial hand washing. He gave this wise reply:

Can't you see that what you eat won't defile you? Food doesn't
come in contact with your heart, but only passes through
the stomach and then comes out again." (By saying this, He
showed that every kind of food is acceptable.) And then He
added, "It is the thought-life that defiles you. For from within,
out of a person's heart, come evil thoughts, sexual immorality,
theft, murder, adultery, greed, wickedness, deceit, eagerness
for lustful pleasure, envy, slander, pride, and foolishness. All
these vile things come from within; they are what defile you and
make you unacceptable to God."   Mark 7:18—23
(NLT)

This is important! The vile things that come out of us originate in the
heart. When a person is involved with sexual immorality, it is because
the heart is focused on self.

{Sin always takes you farther than you ever want to go.}

The good man out of the good treasure of his heart brings forth
what is good; and the evil man out of the evil treasure brings

forth what is evil; for his mouth speaks from that which fills his
heart. Luke 6:45

But the things that proceed out of the mouth come from the
heart, and those defile the man. For out of the heart come
evil thoughts, murders, adulteries, fornications, thefts, false
witness, slander. Matthew 15:18—19

CHAPTER 6
The Heart of Sexual Immorality

When individuals indulge in sexual immorality it is because their heart is focused on having their perceived needs met. As in the diagram, the heart is set on self, getting what *I* want, doing what feels good to *me*, and fulfilling *my* desires.

God Let Them... Romans 1:24

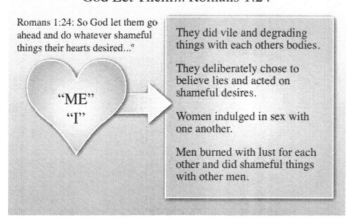

Romans 1:24: So God let them go ahead and do whatever shameful things their hearts desired...°

"ME"
"I"

They did vile and degrading things with each others bodies.

They deliberately chose to believe lies and acted on shameful desires.

Women indulged in sex with one another.

Men burned with lust for each other and did shameful things with other men.

Their thoughts are focused on gratifying their immoral desires, or lusty thoughts, beliefs and desires. They believe they must satisfy the ache or the longing, and often they believe they are not hurting anyone in the process.

Depending on their upbringing, they may believe that pornography and masturbation are an acceptable solution to meet their needs. What is important to them is to have these perceived needs met. Whether they realize it or not, they are placing the desires of their own hearts above everything else.

When a person begins to live for the desires of their own heart, a cascade of sin begins to take place. Little thought is given to the damage they are doing to their conscience in this process.

All that seems to matter is satisfying the lust of the flesh.

Romans 1 is about refusing to honor God as God and the consequences of unrighteousness and ungodliness.

In context, it is applicable to the unbeliever; however, we can still watch the same downward spiral take place in the lives of believers who indulge in various aspects of sexual immorality.

Before engaging in sexual immorality, there is a desire for illicit pleasure. Before a man gets a lap dance at the strip club, there is a belief that he is entitled to what he wants and a belief that he will not get caught. Before the adulterous affair, she had a desire to "be happy," to have her needs met, to feel desired by her cohort.

God Let Them... Romans 1

Romans 1:24: God abandoned them to their evil minds and let them do things that should never be done..."

"ME"
"I"

Their lives became full of:

Every kind of wickedness

Sin

Greed

Murder

Deception

Malicious behavior

Forever inventing new ways of sinning

While God never abandons the believer, He does allow them to experience the consequences of their sexual immorality.

Having counseled people who were involved in an immoral relationship, they inevitably say to me that they can't believe what they have done. They never thought they could sink so low.

The heart that is focused on self does not set out to be depraved; these actions that you see are results. They are not the cause of the problem;

they are what flow over from the heart of man into their lives.
Every perverted and immoral action begins as a thought, the thought is fueled by a desire or a belief, and the desire or belief begins in the heart.

As a man thinks in his heart, so is he. Proverbs 23:7 (NLT)

There is no doubt that our thoughts direct the course of our lives. We base our actions on what we think in the moment and over longer periods of time. The thought life is on display in the life of a person who has been involved in sexual immorality. They have done things that reflect the reality of the Proverb; their thoughts have led to actions that reveal what lurks in the darkness of their heart. Their actions bear testimony to the contents of their heart.

Allow me to explain this using a word picture that has been quite effective:

The Tree of Life
Citrus growers know that the quality of the fruit of any tree depends on the root system of the tree. When the roots are growing in deep, rich soil full of nutrients, the tree will be strong and healthy. The fruit of that tree will be juicy, sweet, and resistant to bugs and parasites.

The tree rooted in poor quality soil will have little nutrition to carry up through the trunk to the branches and leaves. The tree will be weak and susceptible to disease. The quality of its fruit will be poor. We could return year after year and pluck the poor fruit from the tree, but that would not change the health of the tree. The tree would remain sickly and vulnerable, bearing bad fruit. The only way to cause a tree to produce good fruit is to attend to the roots.

To make application to life, if only the visible problems are addressed (fruit), the person will soon return to these problems and feelings in a short time.

What we see as the problem (pornography, adultery, masturbation, deception) is not the real issue; it is a symptom. There is a problem to deal with deeper down in the tree of life; *something* has caused the fruit to be bad.

We must address the root system because that is where the problem truly begins. The person who is involved in sexual sin needs to deal with their lust and sinful desires by attacking the real causes (roots) in a biblical manner. They have to deal with the heart of their problem in order to overcome it.

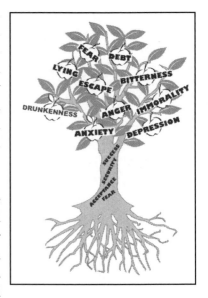

For example, when a person has the fruit of adultery, they have focused their heart on their wants, their perceived needs, their personal rights, their beliefs, and their desires. This results in a self-centered idolatrous heart, which is revealed by their thoughts, words, and actions.

The quality of the fruit of a tree is determined by its root system, and similarly, the condition of the heart will be visible by words and deeds. If the roots of a tree are sunk in fertilized ground that is enriched and full of nutrients, the tree will be strong and its fruit will be good. If the roots are sunk in bad soil and fertilized with poor quality additives or none at all, the roots will have little nutrition to carry up through the trunk to the branches and leaves. The tree will be weak and the quality of its fruit will be poor.

Let us use sexual immorality as fruit. Going back to the reasons why fruit is either of good or bad quality, we must conclude that there is a problem to deal with deeper down in that person's tree of life. Something has caused their fruit to be bad so we must return to the root system.

In the case of humanity, we can say that the root system is equal to the heart. What this means is when someone has the fruit of sexual immorality their roots are embedded in a heart that is not focused on glorifying God. Instead, it is focused on their wants, perceived needs, personal rights, beliefs, and desires. God calls it idolatry when the heart is not focused on Him but instead is focused on something else.

What guides and motivates the heart is what changes the actions and the resulting fruit. When thoughts, beliefs, and desires are set on glorifying God, there will be appropriate actions and God-honoring consequences.

When the heart is set on pleasing "self," thoughts and actions are not naturally going to be like God's. This presents a dilemma, because God commands us in the Bible to be holy.

> *But now you must be holy in everything you do, just as God— who chose you to be His children—is holy. For He Himself has said, "You must be holy because I am holy."*
>
> *1 Peter 1:15—16 (NLT)*

Practicing holiness brings God glory. Glorifying God should be the goal of our lives. Glorifying God happens when the focus of life changes from living for my pleasure and glory to living for His pleasure and glory. It demands that my heart change from a "me" centered focus to a God-centered focus.

In order to accomplish this goal, changes must take place. The first change that must take place is in the heart itself. No one can change their own heart. Because the heart is deceitful and wicked (Jeremiah 17:9), it is not possible to know the depths of its depravity. A person cannot conjure up enough goodness within themselves to change in a real and lasting way.

Many people who have been called sex addicts have tried to change themselves through a New Year's Resolution or a "self-help" group of some kind. The behavior may have changed for a while or to some degree, but studies bear out the fact that merely altering behavior does not bring about lasting and permanent change.

Every issue a person deals with in life, including all forms of sexual immorality, is common to man (1 Corinthians 10:13), and every issue can and must be dealt with on the heart level.

Created to Worship

We have been created to worship. When God made the world and everything in it, His sole reason for doing so is that creation would worship Him and give Him glory.

> *Fear God, and give Him glory ...worship Him who made the heaven and the earth and sea and springs of waters.*
>
> Revelation 14:7

Numerous times in the Psalms we are told to worship the Lord alone, (Psalms 29:2; 66:4; 86:9—10; 95:6; 96:9) and we are commanded to put idols away from us (1 Kings 12:30; 2 Chronicles 7:19—22; Psalm 81:9; 97:7). Over and over again in Scripture, God is telling people to stop worshiping other gods and to worship Him alone!

God spends a *lot* of time in the Bible instructing His people on how important it is that they neither worship other gods, nor make graven images to bow down and worship.

> *You shall have no other gods before Me. You shall not make for yourself an idol, or any likeness of what is in heaven above or on the earth beneath or in the water under the earth. You shall not worship them or serve them; for I, the LORD your God, am a jealous God.*
>
> Exodus 20:3—5a

He tells us that He is a jealous God and will not tolerate the worship of anything or anyone other than Himself. Why does God spend so much time warning us over and over about the worship of idols and other gods? He warns us because each of us struggles with the horrendous sin of idolatry on a daily basis. It is reflected in our choices, our words, our use of time, and how we spend our money. In our culture we tend to think of idolatry as a part of an Eastern religious system such as Buddhism or Hinduism, or as pagan worship of the trees and animals. But the truth is, idolatry is not only bowing down to statues—it is anything that means more to you than God. It is manifested when getting what you want has become more important than what God desires for you. Simply put, anything you love, desire, or serve more than God is an idol of the heart. We are constantly tempted to sin in this manner.

While many technological advances exist in the world, including new things to idolize and worship, Satan uses the same tricks and methods to bait the trap that he has employed since the Garden of Eden. Adam and Eve succumbed to the lust of the eyes, the lust of the flesh, and the pride of life (cf. 1 John 2:16). Sin and guilt entered the world, and Satan has not changed his tactics—ever.

He was so prideful that he actually tried to use the same tactics on the Lord Jesus!

Jesus, full of the Holy Spirit, returned from the Jordan and was led around by the Spirit in the wilderness for forty days, being tempted by the devil. And He ate nothing during those days, and when they had ended, He became hungry. And the devil said to Him, "If You are the Son of God, tell this stone to become bread." And Jesus answered him, "It is written, 'Man shall not live on bread alone.'"

And he led Him up and showed Him all the kingdoms of the world in a moment of time. And the devil said to Him, "I will give You all this domain and its glory; for it has been handed over to me, and I give it to whomever I wish. "Therefore if You worship before me, it shall all be Yours." Jesus answered him, "It is written, 'You shall worship the Lord your God and serve Him only.'" Luke 4:1—8

To this day, Satan uses the same tactics against us. We see this reiterated in John's first epistle to the churches.

For the world offers only the lust for physical pleasure, the lust for everything we see, and pride in our possessions. These are not from the Father. They are from this evil world. 1 John 2:16 (NLT)

Sexual immorality is idolatry. A person who is involved in sexual sin is worshiping the idols of their heart.

Idolatry of the Heart
We have been created to worship God, but our sinful lusts have driven us to worship and idolize the things of the world.

Are you beginning to see how lust, immoral desires, adultery, homosexuality and other sexual struggles proceed from an idolatrous and self-centered heart? At some point in their life, individuals involved in sexual sin of any kind came to believe that they needed certain things or people to "make them happy." For some it provides a feeling of success or security; for others it is acceptance, and for still others it is motivated by power and control, intending to provoke fear.

These motivations, spurred on by the desires of the heart, have born exactly the kind of awful fruit you would expect to see.

Serving God alone means that we deny our urge to idolize things and people. God made things available for us to enjoy and placed people in our lives to love because this glorifies Him. We are not to worship or use these gifts to satisfy our sinful feelings and desires.

THE HEART OF IDOLATRY

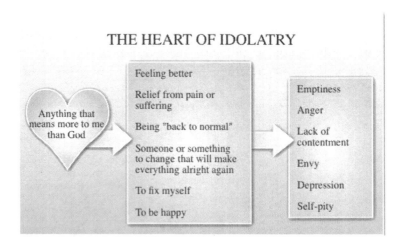

Anything that means more to me than God	Feeling better
	Relief from pain or suffering
	Being "back to normal"
	Someone or something to change that will make everything alright again
	To fix myself
	To be happy

Emptiness
Anger
Lack of contentment
Envy
Depression
Self-pity

As you may have already discovered, when a person's goals, dreams, and desires are in conflict with God's, there will be sorrow. God's desire for us is to glorify Him by living a life that honors and serves Him.

Whatever a person worships or places a high value on is what they serve and obey.

God hates idolatry.

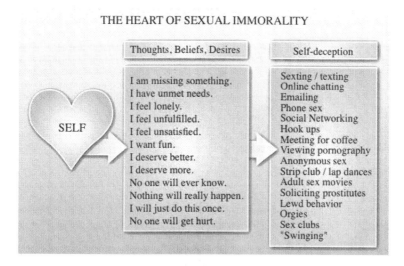

THE HEART OF SEXUAL IMMORALITY

Thoughts, Beliefs, Desires	Self-deception
SELF	
I am missing something. I have unmet needs. I feel lonely. I feel unfulfilled. I feel unsatisfied. I want fun. I deserve better. I deserve more. No one will ever know. Nothing will really happen. I will just do this once. No one will get hurt.	Sexting / texting Online chatting Emailing Phone sex Social Networking Hook ups Meeting for coffee Viewing pornography Anonymous sex Strip club / lap dances Adult sex movies Soliciting prostitutes Lewd behavior Orgies Sex clubs "Swinging"

Having sexual desires is not wrong and those desires themselves are not sinful. God created us to be sexual people! It is important to understand that sexual desires are not evil. However, the thoughts that produce them certainly can be evil and sinful, especially when they are immoral or lust-filled thoughts and desires that cannot be legitimately fulfilled inside of marriage.

Sexual desires within marriage can become sinful when they become idols of the heart. If sexual desires and fulfillment come to mean more to a person than living life to glorify, worship, and serve God, as well as minister to others, they have become idols.

When having felt or physical needs met becomes so important to a person that they are willing to violate God's Word to have them, they have crossed the line from desire to worship. It is a good indication that idolatry is present when we are willing to sin to get what we want.

Do not let your heart turn aside to her ways; do not stray into her paths. Proverbs 7:25

75

Now you have a better understanding of why Scripture speaks so plainly about the heart and how it guides our lives. At its core, the heart is sinful and desperately wicked (Jeremiah 17:9), so it should not surprise us that lust and deception live there.

Each of us struggles with the horrendous sin of idolatry on a daily basis. As Galatians 5 tells us, idolatry is a desire of our sinful nature (flesh). It is reflected in our choices: our words, our use of time, what or who we spend our money on, and where.

Now the deeds of the flesh are evident, which are: immorality, impurity, sensuality, idolatry . . . Galatians 5:19—20a

Are you seeing the pattern here? The sexually immoral person is an idolater who worships the god of self.

Be Careful Little Eyes What You See...

We can thank our cultural predecessors for the current state of society which encourages us to live by our feelings and to immerse ourselves in feeling good. It is now socially and medically accepted that if you feel bad you can artificially boost your feelings and emotions by taking various psychotropic drugs engineered for the sole purpose of altering a person's mood and elevating their feelings.

Music encourages us to do what pleases us and to "do it, do it 'til you're satisfied (whatever it is)."[17] Reality television and movies are *full* of encouragement to do what makes you happy in life, at any cost. As this feeds into the hearts and minds of people, it also aids the heart in rationalizing and justifying its sinful desires.

We have become a society that lives for pleasure and gives little thought to consequences. Those who have been sexually immoral reap for themselves a world of hurt and take their spouses and families along for the ride.

We have returned to the days where everyone does what is right in their own eyes (Judges 17:6) and there is no fear of God or His judgment. Hence, sexual sin is even sought after in the light of day without fear or concern because the conscience has been seared among the men and women of our day.

There is an entire set of idolatrous beliefs that are present in the heart of a person involved in sexual sin. These lies (and others like them) are what a man tells himself that set him up for the immoral woman to move into his heart.

CHAPTER 7

Beware the Immoral One

For many are the victims she has cast down, and numerous are all her slain. Her house is the way to Sheol, descending to the chambers of death.　　　　　　　　　　　　　　　　　　　　　Proverbs 7:26—27

I have included this section on the immoral woman and man because I have found many Christians do not understand what kind of a person could act this way. Scripture tells us about the character and actions of a man or woman involved with sexual sin.

The Immoral Woman
Scripture is brilliantly accurate in its description of the immoral woman, or harlot, as she is called. In the vernacular we would call her a whore. She is a woman who covets another woman's husband.

Characteristics of the Immoral Woman	Scripture Verse/Passage
seductive words	Proverbs 2:16
promiscuous	Proverbs 2:16
abandoned her husband	Proverbs 2:17
ignores the covenant she made before God	Proverbs 2:17
lips are as sweet as honey, her mouth is smoother than oil—as bitter as poison, as dangerous as a double-edged sword.	Proverbs 5:3—4
her feet go down to death; her steps lead straight to the grave	Proverbs 5:5
she cares nothing about the path to life	Proverbs 5:6
her ways are unstable	Proverbs 5:6
the evil woman	Proverbs 6:24
smooth tongue	Proverbs 6:24
hunts for the precious life	Proverbs 6:26

Characteristics of the Immoral Woman	Scripture Verse/Passage
flatters with her words	Proverbs 7:5
cunning of heart	Proverbs 7:5
boisterous (brash) and rebellious	Proverbs 7:6
never content to stay at home	Proverbs 7:11
brazen (brash, shameless) face	Proverbs 7:13
many persuasions, flattering lips	Proverbs 7:21
deep pit, a dangerous trap	Proverbs 23:27
dangerous as falling into a narrow well	Proverbs 23:27
hides and waits like a robber	Proverbs 23:28
says, "I have done no wrong."	Proverbs 30:20
an adulterous woman consumes a man	Proverbs 30:20
boisterous, naive and knows nothing	Proverbs 9:13

An immoral woman is a predator, and she is literally hunting for a man to seduce. In order to capture a man she will use any means necessary to trap him, such as deception, flattery, and sympathy ploys. She hides her true intentions from him by telling him she is looking for a friend, how he is a good listener, or that he understands her like no one else does. She laughs at his jokes and treats him like he is the best man she has ever met. She may talk about how lonely she is, and she acts as though she needs him and wants him more than anyone else ever could. She may be loud and boisterous, acting as though she is happy and having fun in what she has chosen as a lifestyle. She may tell the man that he is the perfect remedy for her loneliness.

> She knew more about him at that time than I did. Hurt, shame, and anger are all a part of my life right now. Wounded, wounded person I am...
>
> *~Christine, wife of John*

She may even use his religion or faith in her quest to capture him. She may use fractured theology and spiritual terminology to identify with him, but she will twist the truth and interject spin and lies to suit her agenda. She targets married men because she wants to feel safe and stable. His religion only adds to the desirability.

The adulteress may tell him stories intended to cause him to want to protect and shelter her from harm or evil. She spins webs of deceit or tells tales of past abuse by her father, another relative, a past husband or boyfriend. This is calculated and intentional on her part. She knows it is his nature to want to protect a woman from harm.

She feeds his pride with compliments about his appearance and wit. Because she has no shame, she is not afraid to speak sexually to him, seducing him with words of desire and promise of indulging his every fantasy. Her skimpy or revealing clothing feeds the lust of the eye and she is not hesitant to flaunt her body in front of him.

This kind of woman wants to know her competition, so she will ask him about his wife and family. She will skillfully pry information from him about his marriage and relationship with his wife. She will be interested in you, his wife. She wants to know your likes and dislikes, your schedule, your activities and your habits. Every question is like a test balloon, and she will monitor his every response and adjust her dialogue to subtly paint you in the worst possible light and herself in the most favorable light. She will capitalize on anything he says that is even remotely negative about you and seek to fill the voids you have left in your marriage.

> What hurt me so very deeply was that he told her about me. He told her things that he never should have told her. He weaponized my deficiencies for her. I know this because that is exactly what she did with the information. It hurt me so deeply that I was a discussion between my husband and his whore. God, that still kills me. It still kills me inside. What a betrayal. What a betrayal....
>
> ~Debbie, wife of Victor

She may ask him to keep their "friendship" a secret, telling him others would not understand. At some point she will offer herself to him physically. It may be a kiss, or an offer for a sexual act. If he hesitates to take the poisonous bait she will assure him that no one will ever know; their relationship will never be found out. She promises it will be "just this once."

These women are reckless and self-centered, void of conscience. Some know they are headed toward the edge of the cliff but do not care. Their desire is to have their "needs" met, to have what they want, to feel better, to feel "loved" and wanted. They are willing to go to any lengths to have what they want, and what they want right now is *your* husband.

> Part of what makes me so angry is what I know she said to him. All the subtle things she wove into conversations about MY deficiencies that added to his dissatisfaction with me. She tried to get him to keep her as his lover and me as his wife.
>
> *~Debbie, wife of Victor*

Beware the Immoral Man

While men can also be immoral and can be equally guilty of adultery, Scripture does not give us as many vivid descriptions of men as it does women.

Characteristics of the Immoral Man	Scripture Verse/Passage
he lies with a man as a woman	Leviticus 20:13
orgies, sexual immorality and sensuality	Romans 13:11–14
looks lustfully at a woman	Matthew 5:28
sexually immoral, idolaters, adulterers, homosexuals	1 Corinthians 6:9–10
joined to a prostitute	1 Corinthians 6:13–20
indulging in youthful passions	2 Timothy 2:22

Characteristics of the Immoral Man	Scripture Verse/Passage
looks with lustful intent/adultery at heart	Matthew 5:27,28
sexual immorality, impurity, passion, evil desire, and covetousness, which is idolatry.	Colossians 3:5
sexual immorality and pursuit of unnatural desire	Jude 1:7
sexual immorality, impurity, sensuality, idolatry	Galatians 5:19–21
a man has his father's wife	1 Corinthians 5:21
violating a virgin	Deuteronomy 22:28–29
incest	2 Samuel 13:1–21
wandering eye	Proverbs 27:20

Whether he is seeking a married or an unmarried woman, the immoral man is a promise maker and a promise breaker. He will say whatever it takes to lure her into his bed, but he has no real intention of following through on his word or the promises he makes. He is deceptive and cunning, using sweet words to worm his way into her heart. He is often complimentary of her face and figure, flattering her and building her self-esteem. He will pose himself as a good listener, someone she can talk to. He intends to pretend to meet her emotional needs to get what he wants from her which is nothing but sex.

He usually has no intention of settling down but will promise her the world if she meets his needs.

If she is married, he views her as "safe" because she will not call, nag, or have expectations of him after the encounter. Men who seek married women are often looking for more risky or adventurous sex. He will get the sex he wants and does not have to become emotionally attached to her. Everything is slanted to his advantage; he can play without "pay."

To catch her he will offer her what she is lacking (or thinks she is lacking) in her current relationship. He views her as a challenge, something to conquer. A man who gets a woman to commit adultery gets a real boost to his pride.

Those interested in more than sex may plant subtle lies in how she thinks about her husband. He questions your goodness toward her. He may tell her that he would be better at loving and cherishing her than you will. Sometimes the man will "fall in love" with the woman which leads to further disaster.

> I think I spend too much time thinking about *him*. I never think good or nice thoughts about him, just hateful ones. He used to be my friend! Does this take away time from my spiritual pursuits? Of course it does! I struggle to pray about anything other than keeping him away from us, preserving my marriage, protecting my wife.
>
> ~*David, husband to Portia*

This kind of man is usually very laid back and cavalier about relationships, preferring to keep things loose and fluid. The overwhelming number of men who have illicit sex are completely self-centered and without conscience. He is in it for his own pleasure, and to sate his physical lusts. He has no intention of having a relationship or intimacy, all he wants is sex without commitment.

Regardless of his words, he does not respect her because he is using her for his own gratification.

Taking the Bait

> *With her many persuasions she entices him; with her flattering lips she seduces him. Suddenly he follows her as an ox goes to the slaughter ...*   Proverbs 7:21—22

When we marry, we make a covenant before God with our spouse to be faithful to them. We are agreeing to bind ourselves and commit ourselves to our husband or wife for the rest of our earthly lives. God established this covenant when he brought Eve to Adam in the Garden and said they were "one flesh" (Genesis 2:24). As we learned previously, in the marriage ceremony God is the one sealing the covenant. God takes the marriage covenant very seriously!

> *Because the LORD has been a witness between you and the wife of your youth, against whom you have dealt treacherously, though she is your companion and your wife by covenant. But not one has done so who has a remnant of the Spirit. And what did that one do while he was seeking a godly offspring? Take heed then to your spirit, and let no one deal treacherously against the wife of your youth. "For I hate divorce," says the LORD, the God of Israel, "and him who covers his garment with wrong," says the LORD of hosts. "So take heed to your spirit, that you do not deal treacherously."*
>
> Malachi 2:14—16

When a man/woman takes the bait and consents to an adulterous relationship s/he breaks the covenant that has been made with his/her spouse to be faithful and true to him/her, to keep him/herself set apart only for their spouse, to honor and cherish him/her. The adulterer breaks his/her vow to love their spouse.

Adultery is the antithesis of 1 Corinthians 13; it is not patient, kind or loving. Adultery is self-seeking, selfish, prideful and arrogant. Adultery destroys the oneness God intended in marriage; the exclusiveness of the relationship is blown away as one marriage partner is joined to another person outside of the covenant.

Taking the bait has been described as a runaway train by those who have succumbed to it. Several people interviewed for this book said that they did not believe that anything would really happen. They did not think anything would "come of it." They said they were "just being nice, friendly, caring, or compassionate" to the person they cheated with, up to the point where things "got out of hand." They "never intended to develop feelings" for the other person, "it just happened."

Some described behaviors that were clearly tempting the flesh, and baiting the hook of desire.

Let no one say when he is tempted, "I am being tempted by God"; for God cannot be tempted by evil, and He Himself does not tempt anyone. But each one is tempted when he is carried away and enticed by his own lust. Then when lust has conceived, it gives birth to sin; and when sin is accomplished, it brings forth death. James 1:13–15

"I do promise and covenant, before God and these witnesses, to be thy loving and faithful husband...I promise to love, honor, cherish, and protect you forsaking all others and holding only unto you as long as we both shall live."

-Traditional Marriage Vow

The trap is laid first in the heart where seeds of dissatisfaction are sewn. The dissatisfaction can be on any level of the marriage: emotional, sexual, companionship, time, distance, etc. and is actually a lack of gratitude for the spouse God has given him/her. In his/her heart s/he lusts after something that is perceived to be lacking in his/her spouse.

When I was a child, my uncle took me on his fishing boat and we trolled around the lake looking for a good spot to catch some fish. James 1:13–15 carries that same connotation with respect to sexual sin.

A person has an evil desire of the heart for sexual gratification outside of the acceptable realm of marriage. The evil desire is a temptation they want to satisfy at any cost, so "trolling" begins. It first begins in the thoughts: "I want (fill in the blank). How can I get (fill in the blank)? I could go there, or buy this, or take a drive to (somewhere) or call (someone) . . ." and so on.

The thoughts begin to scheme to acquire the lust of the heart. The person is enticed to sin as the plausibility of the schemes lock in place. To *entice* means "to capture," or "to bait a hook." The more the heart and mind figure out ways to fulfill the lust, the larger and more unavoidable the hook appears to be.

The lust seems to feel as though it takes on a life of its own. Many who have continued down into these murky depths will say the lust almost personifies and that they feel as though they are being literally spoken to by Desire. They tell me that they can hear the smooth and seductive words of Desire and Lust whispering,

> *I was due to offer peace offerings; today I have paid my vows. Therefore I have come out to meet you, to seek your presence earnestly, and I have found you. I have spread my couch with coverings, with colored linens of Egypt. I have sprinkled my bed with myrrh, aloes and cinnamon. Come, let us drink our fill of love until morning; Let us delight ourselves with caresses . . .*
>
> Proverbs 7:14—18

This is the tipping point for those who even try to resist taking the bait. The desires of the heart are so strong, the lust of the flesh is so great, that they crumple under the pressure and are captured by the sexual sin.

> *With her many persuasions she entices him; with her flattering lips she seduces him. Suddenly he follows her as an ox goes to the slaughter, Or as one in fetters to the discipline of a fool, Until an arrow pierces through his liver; As a bird hastens to the snare, So he does not know that it will cost him his life.*
>
> Proverbs 7:21—23

Desire has spread its net in the heart; the man/woman has been tempted and enticed. Once enticement has taken place, the man/woman has essentially taken the bait of the desire of the heart and walked into the sinful situation.

CHAPTER 8
Learning the News

I don't think anyone who has been betrayed ever really forgets how and when they learned of their spouse's sexual infidelity.

Here's a typical example: A woman says she suspected her husband was looking at porn, but when she accessed the history on his computer and saw it with her own eyes it overwhelmed her. She could not concentrate on anything else the rest of the day; she was distracted and spent time crying. She replayed various scenarios in her mind while waiting to confront her husband.

Mitch's dad had porn lying around their house, and I always wondered how his mom could tolerate that. I thought men who viewed porn were total pigs. I could not understand how his mom would let him touch her after looking at that filthy stuff. In my mind, porn is adultery and Mitch knew I would never stand for him looking at porn and then coming to bed with me.

Mitch always said that stuff didn't interest him, that I was all the woman he needed in his life.

The day I learned of his pack of lies I got on the computer to print out a recipe. There was a bunch of spam in the in box, all of it advertising sexual things. I went to the history to find out what sites had been accessed recently and was completely blown away by what I saw. Literally hundreds of pornographic websites had been accessed in the past week! I clicked on a few of the addresses to be sure that it was not a mistake, and I quickly learned that Mitch had not been working late into the evening as he said he was!

I could not believe my eyes! The amount of porn was staggering and the content was shocking. I could tell that he had been accessing harder and harder porn as time went on, and I was sick to my stomach at the vile things I saw, which was not even the worst of it.

As I printed out the browser report I began to think about what I would say to Mitch when he came home that evening. I could not stay married to him if this is what he was going to be doing. I began to plan my exit strategy that day.

~Phyllis, wife of Mitch

When you learned of his/her sexual immorality, you most likely experienced a flood of emotions. I have been told that when a spouse learns of the pornography problem, the adultery, the strip clubs or prostitutes, the emotions swing from paralyzing shock to a desire to commit suicide and/or homicide. There is disbelief and overwhelming rage, crushing pain, grief and sorrow that defy description.

When a woman or man learns their spouse has had a physical affair, everything takes on an unreal quality. It is the worst possible news you can imagine receiving. Some say it is worse than learning you have cancer or some other disease. The only words that can even come close to describing it are utter devastation.

If it is your husband, you most likely want to know all the details. If the sexual immorality is with pornography you will have questions about how long this has been going on and wonder how deep this problem goes. As his wife, you will want to pry inside your husband's mind and learn what drove him to look at those images! You will want to know what exactly he has been thinking of while the two of you were having sex. Who has he been picturing in his mind? Has he been fantasizing about one of the women in those videos while he was physically touching you? You might wonder how he could watch those acts on the computer and still read his Bible or attend church with you.

If you discover it is your wife who has committed physical adultery, watches porn, or had an emotionally adulterous or online relationship, your first response may be rage. You might interrogate your wife and demand to see all the communication between the two of them. You might require her to prove that she has never met with him in person and go through her phone logs to see if they have been talking by phone.

You will want to know the details of her activities. Men seem to want the explicit details of the sexual encounters as much as women do and for the same reasons. Ultimately, you want to know where you didn't measure up to your wife and what drove her into the arms of another man, or what compels her to immerse herself in a cesspool of pornography.

This does not change with the number of years a person is married. There is nothing quite like learning your spouse has broken the covenant and thrown away the commitment made to you.

I could not understand what I was hearing her say. It was like the roar of the ocean in my head. I saw her mouth moving, tears coming down her cheeks, and it sunk in that she was forming the words, "affair" and repeating, "I'm so sorry, I'm so sorry" over and over.

I remember thinking, "This can't be happening. She is not telling me she had an affair, no way. She is not saying these things to me."

But she was. I was struck dumb. I must have looked like a total idiot standing there while she cried and told me she was in love with another man. She asked me if I wanted her to leave, if I was going to divorce her. There was no way I could make decisions like that right then; I needed time to think, to get my head on straight.

~Dan, husband of Maureen

For some, learning of the adultery is a confirmation of something that has been suspected for a long time, and for others, it comes out of nowhere and takes them completely by surprise.

I went into the den and shut the door. Suddenly I found myself full of rage and I destroyed the room. I wiped everything off the shelves, cleared the desk of its contents, hurled the computer across the room into the wall, and took every picture of my "loving family" off the wall and smashed them to bits.

I could hear her on the other side of the door pounding and screaming at me to stop, but believe me, it was better for her that I did not open the door; I would have killed her.

~Andy, husband of Jeanna

I had suspected for a while that there was some truth to the suspicions I had. When the first email came I tried to brush it off but I wondered, "Why would she send me an email like this?" I grilled him pretty hard and checked all his email and Facebook entries. I was more watchful but nothing seemed out of place. He was loving, attentive and life was good. When the second email came and included her phone number I knew it was true.

When he came home from his tennis game I told him I knew about her, that she asked me to call her so there was no sense in denying it anymore. My suspicions did nothing to soften the blow of his admission. I ran to the bathroom and threw up, and then I sank to the floor sobbing.

My hopes and dreams were shattered and I thought my life was over. In that moment I did not care if I lived or died. I wondered how I could have been such a fool to believe him when he had been lying to me for years.

~Shanda, wife of Paul

I want you to know that as much as you want all the details, it is not good for you to know them. What I have been told by those who have experienced this is how knowing all the details only adds to your sorrow and anger.

If your spouse has been physically unfaithful you will need to know certain things, such as the risk of contracting an STD, HIV or some other disease. You will need to know how many physical sexual partners there have been because of the compounding factors involved with sexual histories. These things are to protect you.

For all sexual sin disclosure, you will need to know some of the details for your own peace of mind. You must learn to ask questions. As difficult as this will be for both of you, I urge you to be willing to listen to him/her make a full disclosure of their sin. I know that you think you won't be able to handle it all in one sitting, and for some that is not even possible because of the extent of the transgressions.

However, it is very damaging to think you know everything there is to know and learn months or years down the road that there was unconfessed sin. Allow your spouse to make a full and accurate disclosure to you because it is a part of the accountability for their actions. Some planning and preparation on the part of the offending spouse will make a great deal of difference.

With that in mind, I strongly caution you from trying to force every gritty detail from your spouse; it is not helpful or healthy for you. Knowing these things will give you more things to ruminate on and will give you more reason to justify sinful anger. Accept that there are some things you really do not need to know.

If your spouse is finished with his/her foolishness, his/her thoughts will not be about preserving him/herself; s/he will be thinking of you. If s/he is not willing to end the illicit relationship or get help for their pornography or other sexual sin idolatry, learning these things will only cause you deeper pain.

Each person reacts differently to hearing the news that his/her spouse has been unfaithful. You can do a great amount of damage to what is left of your relationship upon learning of the infidelity, or you can take steps to bring healing into the marriage. By God's grace your marriage can be restored.

CHAPTER 9
Dealing with the Fallout

After you learn of your spouse's infidelity, the first days pass in a fog. Looking back, you may wonder how you went to work, put meals on the table, and spent time with family or friends. If you did, you might ask yourself how you kept everything looking so "normal" on the outside while inside you were eating broken glass.

You may not have responded well at all. You may have spent days in bed doing nothing but crying. You may have thrown him/her out and flung all his/her belongings on the lawn. You may have called a lawyer or bad-mouthed him/her to everyone you know.

The least damage possible is the best avenue of response, especially if you want to fight for and save your marriage.

If you choose to do so, there are some things that you and your husband/wife must be aware of and admit. Your spouse **has** to get honest with him/herself and with you.

They followed the lust of the heart, the lust of their flesh. Your spouse **has** to own that. Until they own it, they think of themselves as a victims of something or someone outside of themselves. They will want to shift the blame from self to another person or thing. This cannot be allowed to stand, as it is rationalization and justification of the sexually immoral actions.

This is very important because the adulterer who wants to think of themselves as a victim of the person who "lured" them, "tricked" them, or "lied" to them is at great risk to repeat their offense because they continue to lie to themselves about the reason they committed sexual sin.

It is part of the sinful nature to want to place the blame solely on the other person; after all, who wants to look at themselves the way one must when they have done something so horrific to the person they claim to love? The adulterer *must* see that at the roots, their sin was not about anything more than fulfilling their sinful, unholy, ungodly desires.

Your husband/wife also had a belief that s/he would not get caught in their sin. This is painful for you as his/her spouse to take in and comprehend. Your husband/wife has promised to be true to you until death, and yet has schemed and plotted ways to deceive you with the full knowledge that what they were doing was wrong.

If it was physical or emotional adultery, s/he made plans to meet their lover in secret, which meant phone calls or emails were exchanged between them. This kind of betrayal is very hard to accept. You might be wondering how you can ever trust him/her again because their word certainly appears to be meaningless!

Equally hard to accept (yet you must) is that s/he most likely dishonored you to his/her lover. S/he told the lover things about you, things that made it easier for him/her to betray you and made it easier for that lover to worm their way into your spouse's heart. These are the things that betrayed spouses find so hurtful.

Regardless of how much your spouse enjoyed their sin in the moment, if your husband/wife is a Christian, there was always a sense of guilt. The sex was never guilt-free, the conversations were never guilt-free, the "love" s/he had for their accomplice was never guilt-free. The thrill from the pornography was never guilt-free. There was always the cloud of guilt, the knowledge that s/he was doing something wrong and had to hide it.

If your husband or wife is a Christian s/he lived in constant fear of being discovered. There is no freedom in adultery or any other sexual sin, and no freedom in any kind in illicit relationships. Everything is done under a thick blanket of secrecy.

These are some of the things that led to the change you saw in your spouse. This is in part why s/he became so quiet, reclusive, distant, or angry. This is why s/he was not available for you when you needed him/her. Immorality takes a lot of planning and mental energy to sustain.

When there is physical adultery, there is also the possibility that at some point in the "relationship" your husband/wife may have thought seriously about ending your marriage and going to be with their lover. This creates a huge amount of strain and internal strife.

The fallout from your spouse's revelation will vary greatly depending on various contingencies.

- If your spouse is or is not repentant
- If your spouse is or is not willing to radically amputate the sin from their life
- If you and your spouse are or are not interested in reconciliation
- Your financial status
- If you have children or not
- If the sexual sin was criminal—sexual assault, incest, child pornography, rape, voyeurism, solicitation of a prostitute, solicitation of a child for sex

These are also a few of the considerations that people use to help them to decide how or if to go on after the truth is revealed.

Anger

Ephesians 4:26 says to "be angry and do not sin."

The Bible teaches us anger is not sinful in and of itself, for God says He is angry with the wicked every day (Psalm 7:11). A perfectly holy God cannot sin.

Anger is part of the emotional package God has given to each human being. If we did not have anger we could not know joy or peace. If we did not get angry we could not understand the need for forgiveness.

God intends the emotion of anger to motivate us to correct wrongs and injustices. He intends for us to use it positively and for good as the Lord Jesus Christ did when clearing the money changers out of the temple (John 2:13–22). Jesus also was frequently angry with the Pharisees about their hypocrisy (Matthew 23) and the hardness of their hearts (Mark 3:5).

Righteous anger is a Christ-like response that comes from knowing a command or biblical principle has been violated. Anger at sexual sin is righteous, as is being angry at anything else that is in complete conflict with God's commands.

When David sinned with Bathsheba (2 Samuel 11), he also sinned against Uriah. However, he recognized that his primary sin was against the Holy God. Note his admission to God in the verses below:

> *Against you only have I sinned.*   Psalm 51:4

> *As for me, I said, "O LORD, be gracious to me; Heal my soul, for I have sinned against You."*   Psalm 41:4

In committing adultery, your husband/wife broke the covenant made before God when you were married. S/he promised to keep him/herself only for you for the rest of your lives. Your husband/wife has first and foremost sinned against God. Righteous anger is born out of a passion when what is right and holy has been violated, *not* how that sin affects *you*. This is why it is difficult to be righteously angry when betrayed.

As I said previously, your spouse's adultery will provoke a variety of emotions within you. One of those emotions will be anger. Therefore, you will have aspects of both righteous and unrighteous anger.

THE HEART OF ANGER

"I"
"ME"

I want my way

I want relief from suf-fering

Someone or something to change that will make everything alright again

To control others

To control God

I have a right

Bitterness

Loneliness

Lack of contentment

Envy

Depression

Self-pity

While a sinfully angry response to marital infidelity is humanly understandable, we can never excuse or justify sin. Pain tends to cause a person to draw inward and to focus on self. A betrayed spouse often verbalizes many of the thoughts and desires in the diagram below. These kinds of thoughts are what fuel sinfully angry responses and can ruin what is left of the marriage relationship. Sinful anger is at the root, which is a heart issue.

Galatians 5:20 lists anger, strife, disputes, dissentions, enmity, all as deeds of the flesh; all of these are heart issues and displayed as fruit in a person's life. The Bible is clear on God's command to put away this destructive feeling and emotion on the heart level.

> *Let all bitterness and wrath and anger and clamor and slander be put away from you, along with all malice.*
> Ephesians 4:31

One of the methods often used to deal with anger is to stuff it away inside. This is fairly common among Christians, because it is commonly believed that if anger is not visible it is not there. Since s/he does not appear to be angry or upset over the spouse's sexual sin they are thought of as having tremendous self-control. While that may be partially true (because they are practicing some measure of restraint), often they are being eaten away on the inside as they attempt to control and hold down the rage that lives within them.

The *emotion* must be addressed biblically or there will be no resolution to the matter in the heart. Further complicating problems will result.

Internalized anger tends to breed headaches, stomach and intestinal problems, muscular tightness and bodily aches and pain. Angry people also may seek acceptable ways to release their anger through disguised means like sarcasm, friendly insults and biting humor. Some people will stuff it all inside for days, weeks or months until one day, something seemingly small happens and they just explode or emotionally collapse.

An angry person is focused only on self and not on others; most important, his/her focus is not on God. You must deal with your anger on the heart level because any attempts to deal with only the results or the emotion of anger will be *temporary* and in the long run ineffective. You will have to examine the heart-attitudes that motivate and feed your anger.

Typically because of the pain-related self-focus there is a great sense of injustice at what has been done to you, your children, your dreams for your marriage and even your life. If you look back to the diagram on the Heart of Idolatry (page 64) you will see that many of your present thoughts, beliefs, and desires are similar or the same as those found there. The heart of anger and the heart of idolatry have much in common! In both cases feeling better, having relief from pain or suffering, to be happy, and for everything to be alright again are a major focus. These desires bring emptiness, a lack of contentment in your circumstances, and envy at the whole and happy marriages around you. These in turn foster self-pity and can lead to depression.

Bitterness

Anger is a cousin to bitterness. Bitterness could be defined as perpetual anger for how you have been sinned against, or because you believe God is dealing with you unfairly. You should know that if you fail to address your anger biblically or to deal with it at all the result will be bitterness in your heart that will poison every aspect of your life.

If you are bitter, you most likely feel justified in your bitterness because your spouse has done you wrong. Perhaps you find yourself thinking and saying things like, "Under these circumstances, can you blame me?" This reflects a victim mentality and you may not see a reason to stop your bitterness toward your husband or wife. Furthermore, you may hold your spouse responsible for your bitterness. After all, if s/he would never have been involved in sexual sin, you would have no reason to be bitter, right? Bitter people do not see bitterness as something to feel guilty about because it was something done to them—hence, the bitterness is justified.

I understand that you have been sinned against and that you have deep pain and grief. I know that even now your husband/wife may be in the midst of sexual sin or has not yet repented, adding to the sorrow you feel.

As difficult as it will be, you must take your focus off of your hurt, betrayal and anger at his/her sin. Begin to look at what God intends to do in and through this whole situation.

Scripture tells us:

> *Do not let sin control the way you live; do not give in to its lustful desires. Do not let any part of your body become a tool of wickedness, to be used for sinning. Instead, give yourselves completely to God since you have been given new life. And use your whole body as a tool to do what is right for the glory of God.*   Romans 6:12—13 (NLT)

When you sin in your anger you use your body as a tool of wickedness—whether you are exploding with anger, using your tongue or hands, or internalizing it by stuffing it inside.

There will indeed be struggles as you wrestle with your thoughts, desires and emotions, but remember that Christ is the way to victory. You are able through the power of the Holy Spirit to deny yourself and learn to respond differently.

> *... prepare your minds for service and be self-controlled.*
>   1 Peter 1:13

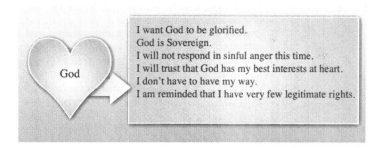

You will have to prepare your mind for battle against the usual thoughts, beliefs, and desires that lead you to become angry at your husband/wife. Because of the depth of the pain your flesh is not going to lie down quietly; you have to have a biblical plan of action and meditate on that in your heart instead of cherishing the hurt and the betrayal.

Remember that what drives the anger is your thoughts, beliefs and desires about this situation. The more you dwell on what has been done to you, the betrayal you have suffered, and the loss you have incurred, the deeper the roots of anger and bitterness grow. This becomes a circular thinking pattern that, if left unchecked, will only grow more difficult to overcome with time.

You must begin to renew your mind (Romans 12:2) with God's truth. The Lord does not instruct us to deny the pain of adultery or other sexual sin, but to view it as He does. Sexual sin is not unforgivable! The person who commits sexual sin can be washed whiter than snow (Isaiah 1:18) and be pure in the eyes of God.

Ask for God's help to accept that He looks upon sexual sin and sexual sinners as He does any other sin or sinner. His desire is that men and women would repent of sexual sin and live in a way that brings Him honor and glory both in the inner and outer man. If your spouse has repented of his/her sin, s/he is most likely already making changes in his/her life intended to bring God glory.

I would also suggest you plan *how* to respond biblically when you want to become angry. One way to do that would be to research

Bible verses that address the specific trigger issues that anger you. Post those verses in places that are easily visible in the moment of need, such as on your computer monitor, refrigerator, dash board, or bedroom mirror.

You might consider carrying around a small card that says **"Does this _____glorify God?"** This small reminder can help you to center your thoughts on glorifying God all day long.

The focus of your heart and life must change from *self* and your anger toward God and His forgiveness, righteousness and holiness. This may require you to tell yourself that it is not alright to sin in your anger. You need to accept that God has purposefully and intentionally designed this trial for you and your spouse.

I strongly urge you to begin to study about the sovereignty of God[18] to gain wisdom and understanding of the plan of God for your life going forward.

CHAPTER 10
The Biblical Response

Forgiveness

I have often heard it said, "I can forgive anything except adultery." Adultery and other kinds of physical sexual sin violate the most closely held tenats of marriage and are among the hardest to forgive. There is nothing quite as challenging as forgiving intentional sin. When a husband/wife is asked to consider forgiving sexual sin, the challenge factor goes up astronomically.

If you intend to deal biblically with the fallout of the sexual sin in which your husband/wife has been involved, you will have to understand what it means to forgive him/her biblically and how to do so.

> *So, as those who have been chosen of God, holy and beloved, put on a heart of compassion, kindness, humility, gentleness and patience; bearing with one another, and forgiving each other, whoever has a complaint against anyone; just as the Lord forgave you, so also should you.*
>
> Colossians 3:12—13

I am not sure I can forgive

When it comes to forgiving sexual sin, one of the major reasons a husband/wife may not want to forgive is because they believe the hurt and betrayal are just too big to get past. Sexual sin is the unforgivable sin in marriage in the minds of many people; however, is that what the Bible teaches?

Many people struggle to forgive in general because they are not clear about what forgiveness from the heart really is; they do understand and look for reasons or make excuses not to forgive.

The Bible teaches us that the greatest need we all have is to be forgiven for our sin. Without the forgiveness of sin we are all destined for hell and eternal damnation (Romans 6:23). You don't have to be Bible a scholar to figure out that if God forgives us, He has the expectation that we will forgive each other on the basis of the forgiveness we've received.

To refuse to forgive will add to the internal misery and woe you will experience. The unforgiving person is the one who suffers the most. If you choose not to forgive, I *guarantee* you will become bitter. If you choose this path, you may as well know right up front that you are deliberately enslaving yourself. The sins of bitterness and unforgiveness enslave you and will ruin your life. You may think that by refusing to forgive the offending spouse will "get theirs," but that is not so. If you refuse to forgive, you will be the one who suffers even greater misery than you have experienced as a result of his/her sexual sin.

I have also been told by a wife that she can't forgive her husband until she forgets what he did. This is backward thinking and is indicative of someone who is holding on to the wrong that has been done to them. Each time she chooses to dwell on the offense and the hurt she has experienced, she engrains it a little deeper in her mind and heart. As I've said elsewhere in this book, there is no way that a person can heal by meditating on the wrong done to them.

The truth is that every time you choose to dwell on the offense and hurt, you obviously are not going to forgot about it. In fact, rehearsing the offense only serves to exacerbate the pain which in turn leads to bitterness. You will not forget until you learn to forgive. When you forgive the wrong done to you, you release it and then, in time, you will begin to forget.

Some husbands/wives remain angry and unforgiving because their spouse has not asked to be forgiven. They say, "I'll forgive when s/he says they are sorry."

Jesus teaches on forgiveness
The Lord addresses this with Peter in Matthew 18. Peter thought he was being very generous by boasting that he would forgive the same man seven times. The Lord Jesus revealed his heart by instructing him to forgive 70 times seven!
The same instruction was given in Luke:

> *Be on your guard! If your brother sins, rebuke him; and if he repents, forgive him. And if he sins against you seven times a*

day, and returns to you seven times, saying, 'I repent,' forgive him.   Luke 17:3—4

At first glance it appears that granting forgiveness is conditioned on the person actually asking for it first. Some spouses are reluctant to forgive because their husband/wife has not asked them for forgiveness nor have they repented of their sexual sin.

The argument goes something like this: "God forgives us when we ask for forgiveness and repent of our sin." In other words, God's forgiveness is conditional in some sense and not unilaterally applied to everyone whether they ask for it or not. This is certainly true in a salvific sense. God does not forgive everyone, everywhere for all their sins—only those who trust in Christ and His finished work on the Cross are forgiven.

The reasoning here goes one step further and applies God's type of forgiveness to human relationships. It suggests that unless someone asks for forgiveness, you can never really forgive them because without them asking, there isn't any taking ownership of their sin as one would when repenting to God.

This, too, is true as far as it goes. Unless a person asks, obviously there is no admission of sin; however, that does not that mean we are free to withhold forgiveness.

The Bible says we are to forgive. I've had professing Christians tell me that the Bible is nice but it's not realistic. The first thing you must understand is that forgiving your spouse is not an option for the Christian; it is required.

We are to follow the example of Christ Jesus, who, while He hung on the cross, being crucified for crimes He did not commit, said:

> *"Father, forgive them; for they do not know what they are doing." And they cast lots, dividing up His garments among themselves.*   Luke 23:34

The son of God was being cruelly and unjustly crucified. The Romans who were performing the deed were casting lots for his garments, and some of His last words were words of forgiveness. In other words, Jesus was saying, "Father, don't hold this against them."

Jesus, it would seem, was practicing the very teaching He shared with His disciples:

> For this reason the kingdom of heaven may be compared to a king who wished to settle accounts with his slaves. When he had begun to settle them, one who owed him ten thousand talents was brought to him. But since he did not have the means to repay, his lord commanded him to be sold, along with his wife and children and all that he had, and repayment to be made. "So the slave fell to the ground and prostrated himself before him, saying, "Have patience with me and I will repay you everything." And the lord of that slave felt compassion and released him and forgave him the debt.
>
> Matthew 18:23–27

Jesus says this is what it is like in God's world—the kingdom of heaven. The king wishes to settle accounts and the man in question owes a very, very large sum—a sum so large there is no way he could pay it back. The word "talent" is a word of weight, not worth, for a talent of gold was worth more than a talent of silver. But the sheer number of talents (think a billion US dollars) clearly makes this a staggering sum that the guy is not going to be able to pay back.

At first, the king seeks justice and commands the man and his family be sold into slavery so that some sort of repayment is made, even though it would be only a very small drop in a very large bucket. The servant realizes this is not going well, so he begs for mercy and promises to repay what he certainly knows he cannot.

The king overlooks the obvious lie and, moved with compassion, cancels the entire debt, releasing the man from any punishment whatsoever. This then is the key in this story of what it means to extend grace. The kingdom of God is a kingdom of grace—unmerited favor toward sinners who cannot pay back even a fraction of what they truly owe. It's a lie to think we can pay back anything.

Jesus' point is that we are to see ourselves as this first servant: a sinner, saved by grace, who has been forgiven a huge, huge debt and escaped punishment simply because our King is gracious. The point is that we are to forgive on the basis of grace, and if we refuse, we really do not grasp just how unmerited our salvation is.

The Level Ground on Which You Stand

You have to understand that your position before God is exactly level with that of the worst sexual sinner, because the ground is level at the foot of the cross. There is nothing exceptional about you or any non-sexual-sin sinner; this is because we are *all* sinners and all in need of God's grace and mercy. You must choose to forgive your husband/wife on the basis of what God has forgiven you.

God intended to forgive you of your sin before you asked. In fact, He *did* forgive you of your sin at the cross, which was long before you were born. How can you withhold forgiveness from your husband/wife for their sin?

"You don't know what s/he has done!" "If you had my pain, you wouldn't forgive either!" "If I forgive him/her, s/he will only hurt me again!" I have heard these plaintive wails coming from many hurting spouses like you but none of these are acceptable reasons to refuse to forgive.

Remember that you are a sinner who gets into the kingdom not on your merit but by the merit of your Savior. You make a choice to extend grace to others on the basis of the abundance of grace you received.

But I don't feel forgiving!

I have heard many times from counselees that they don't *feel* forgiving. They justify withholding forgiveness based on how they feel rather than operating on a Scriptural basis. There is no command or instruction to forgive when you feel like it. Forgiveness is an act of faith or the will that triumphs over the feeling (i.e. desire) to be unforgiving and seek revenge or remain bitter.

If you wait to *feel* forgiving it may never happen, and you will become bitter, angry and hateful. Your life will become a barren wasteland of ruined relationships and sorrow.

By forgiving your spouse you will choose to release him/her from the sense of debt you believe you are owed because s/he hurt you. It's like saying, "Husband/wife, you do not owe me anything, nor will I personally punish you for what you did to me. I choose to forgive you this debt just as I have been forgiven my enormous debts by God."

This takes *big faith!* In order to exercise big faith, you must believe that you serve a big God who is able to work in all circumstances of life.

What is forgiveness

Forgiveness is a promise you will first make to God that you will not dwell on his/her sin against you. You will promise to resist the urge to meditate on the incident(s). When the memories arise you will put them down and take them captive by God's grace and help in that time of need (1 Corinthians 10:13).

You will also agree that you will treat the sin of your husband/wife as God treats your sin—that you will choose to remember no more the sin that was committed against you (Hebrews 8:12).

This means you do not use the past as a weapon to hurt your husband/ wife when you have the opportunity to do so. In those moments when you are tempted to become angry all over again or to hurl hurtful words and reminders of the sin at your husband or wife, you will choose to close your mouth and open your heart, again remembering the great debt that you have been forgiven by God in Christ. You will chose to think about what is true and real in the present (Philippians 4:8), not the past.

You will also promise not bring it up to others. You will not talk to others about how s/he hurt you, still trying to get your pound of flesh to make them pay. You won't bring it up as a prayer request, on Facebook or anywhere else.

These are some enormous promises to make! I suggest making these promises to God first, and then, once you have done that, speak to your husband/wife about forgiveness. I have found that by the time a spouse is willing to agree with God about forgiveness the healing has already begun and the subsequent discussion with their husband/wife is not as difficult as you would think it should be.

When you speak to your spouse, be sure to choose a time when there is opportunity to talk. Disclose the spiritual journey the Lord has taken you on that brought you to the place of being willing to forgive and give God the glory He is due for bringing forgiveness about in your heart.

When you speak of forgiveness, be sure not to make it conditional, such as: "I forgive you as long as you . . ." Offer forgiveness to him/her the way God offered it to you.

In summary, when forgiving your spouse, it is important to remember a few rules: When you forgive, you resolve never to bring this circumstance or situation up again to the one you forgave, to anyone else, or even to yourself. It is a closed book. If you are going to pattern your forgiveness after that of the Lord, then you will choose to remember no more the sin committed against you.

Repentance

There are many questions regarding repentance and how to know when a person has truly repented of their sexual sin. Knowing this is crucial in helping the spouse of the person who has sinned sexually to begin to trust them again and have any faith that their behavior won't be repeated.

Does your spouse claim to have repented of their sin? Biblically, true repentance is a threefold response to sin that is found in the use of three different words that express a different aspect of repentance. All three components or aspects must be present for there to be fruit of true repentance in a person's life.

The first response of repentance is found in the Greek word metanoeo which means a "change of mind" (Matthew 3:2, Mark 1:15).[19]

When a person has a change of mind it means that s/he has acknowledged their sin. This is what we find when a person confesses their sin. They admit and understand that what they have done is sinful. There is no justification or rationalization attached to the sin, no attempts to minimize or blame shift the responsibility for it onto someone else. There is personal guilt attached to the acts that have been committed.

Repentance cannot stop here because it is incomplete. There are plenty of situations where a person has confessed their sin and admitted their guilt and nothing more happens with them; there is no other visible change and things go back to normal. This means the sin resumes at some point or something else takes its place.

An excellent example of this would be the Pharaoh as he dealt with Moses and the Israelites. Twice he admitted to Moses, "I have sinned against the Lord your God" (Exodus 9:27; 10:16). He admitted he sinned, he did not justify or rationalize or shift the blame, and yet he did not repent. There were no changes that accompanied his admission; in fact, he went right back to his behavior! King Saul had the same kind of limited repentance (1 Samuel 15:24, 24:17; 26:21) and he did not cease in pursuing David no matter how sorry he was. It is clear that just admitting sin does not equal repentance.

The second critical aspect of repentance is *metanolomai* (Matthew 21:29, 32; Hebrews 7:21) and it means "change of heart." In addition to admitting and confessing their sin there must be a change of heart with respect to the sin; what they once loved and worshiped they now hate.

There is no longer room in his/her heart for the lust they sought to fulfill, and there is a growing hatred for everything that led him/her to commit sexual sin in the first place. We could call this a holy hatred and it is an emotional response that is experienced in the body in the form of deep sorrow over their sin.

An important difference must be made here: there is a great difference between worldly sorrow and godly sorrow. Godly sorrow has as its first concern the honor of God. It is other's oriented and is produced by the

Holy Spirit acting on the conscience of a sinner. This kind of sorrow cries out, "Woe is me" and causes a person to weep bitterly over the sin s/he has committed.

When the Apostle Peter denied Christ three times after the arrest of Jesus, he went off and wept (*metanoeo*). He was heartbroken (*metanolomai*) over his sin and over how he had betrayed the One he loved. By comparison, Judas also repented (*metamelomai*), meaning he had a change of heart about betraying an innocent man; he felt guilty about it and sought to rectify his betrayal by returning the money he was paid. His hope was to erase his guilt and somehow undo what he had done. He then went and hung himself (Matthew 27:3—5).

It is important to note that repentance is a manifestation of the life of Christ in a person. It is a proof of salvation in a person's life. The sinner (like Peter in the above example) has been deeply convicted to the heart by the Spirit and/or the Word of God that their sin is grievous to the Lord; because of that they no longer desire to participate in it. Worldly sorrow is "unsanctified remorse"[20] (like Judas in the above example) and is focused on feelings of regret, fear, and even desperation. Its focus is on how the sin or its exposure will affect them. MacArthur further says that worldly sorrow "has no redemptive capability. It is nothing more than the wounded pride of getting caught in a sin and having one's lusts go unfulfilled."[21]

The first two kinds of repentance take place in the inner man, or the heart. This is critical because as the heart is changed, the actions change, which lead us to the third part of this critical aspect of repentance.

Finally, there must be *metanoia*, which is a "change in the course of life" (Matthew 3:8; 9:13; Acts 20:21). We know that the Apostle Peter truly did repent because his life demonstrated all of the aspects of repentance: he understood his sin (fear), he grieved over his sin (fear of man), and his life changed (he boldly proclaimed Christ for the rest of his life, and ultimately was martyred for the faith).

Changing the course of life involves an act of the will, a turning from the sinful behavior. There must be a radical amputation of the actions. In other words, there is no more adultery taking place, the pornography has been disposed of, the Facebook account has been deleted, the email has been closed.

> *If your hand causes you to stumble, cut it off; it is better for you to enter life crippled, than, having your two hands, to go into hell, into the unquenchable fire, [where their worm does not die, and the fire is not quenched.] If your foot causes you to stumble, cut it off; it is better for you to enter life lame, than, having your two feet, to be cast into hell, [where their worm does not die, and the fire is not quenched.] If your eye causes you to stumble, throw it out; it is better for you to enter the kingdom of God with one eye, than, having two eyes, to be cast into hell ...*
>
> Mark 9:43—47

When repentance is genuine you *will* see all of this and the change will be dramatic.
Repentance is not something a person can conjure up from within. No amount of screaming or threatening will force a person to repent. Repentance is a gift from God which is why we must pray diligently for God to grant it.

> *The Lord's bond-servant must not be quarrelsome, but be kind to all, able to teach, patient when wronged, with gentleness correcting those who are in opposition, if perhaps God may grant them repentance leading to the knowledge of the truth, and they may come to their senses and escape from the snare of the devil, having been held captive by him to do his will.*
>
> 2 Timothy 2:24—26

Repentance can come quickly or sometimes will take years, but one thing is for certain: a regenerated Christian *will* repent. There will be no way for him/her to live under the conviction and ministry of the Holy Spirit without repenting.

Or do you think lightly of the riches of His kindness and tolerance and patience, not knowing that the kindness of God leads you to repentance?   *Romans 2:4*

Consequences and Repentance

In the Old Testament, King David is a biblical model study for repentance of and consequences for sexual sin. Much of the sorrow and misery David endured as King was the result of his sexual sin with Bathsheba. He went so far as to plot and commit a murder to cover it up. He did evil to another man's family and in 2 Samuel 12 God lays out the consequences for David's sin—and they were severe.

The child of his adultery died; his daughter Tamar was raped by her brother; his other son Absolom conspired and rebelled against David.

One has only to look at his Psalms to glean the depths of the physical and emotional suffering that can accompany the discipline of God.

Many Christians have read that it is a terrible thing to fall into the hands of the living God (Hebrews 10:31), and those who have been under the discipline of God will tell you it is absolutely true.

David repented as a result of the Holy Spirit's work in his heart and life (Psalm 51). If your spouse is a regenerated believer, that same Spirit will be working within them. I tell you again: if s/he is a Christian, s/he *will* repent.

When God disciplines us it is as His children, not as His enemies. It is God's desire that your spouse repent. In some cases, the spouse who is involved in sexual sin may not be regenerate. It is God's desire that they repent and turn to Him first for salvation.

The Lord is not slow about His promise, as some count slowness, but is patient toward you, not wishing for any to perish but for all to come to repentance.   *2 Peter 3:9*

The Fruit of Repentance

Therefore bear fruits in keeping with repentance.   Luke 3:8a

How will you know if your spouse has truly repented? As I said previously, there will be fruit of the repentance in the form of radical amputation of the sexual sin. Pornography will be willingly disposed of or destroyed. Your spouse will ask for help and accountability in this area; s/he will want to be transparent about their activities.

In cases of emotional or physical adultery, the other woman/man will be cut off completely. There will be no avenue open for conversation, connecting, or meeting on any level. If the adultery is going on when s/he is discovered, one approach to take would be to have the husband/wife listen on the phone when the lover is called and the relationship is ended. All emails, Facebook accounts, Twitter accounts, and cell phones are purged to close every possible means of contact. The perpetrator will literally come clean and do so willingly, despite any discomfort on his/her part. Where there is hesitancy there are areas that lack repentance.

Don't mistake the hesitancy that comes from shame for a lack of repentance; when your husband/wife repents and sees the damage s/he has caused, there is an enormous sense of shame and fear of inflicting further hurt on you and more damage to what is left of your relationship. Ask the Lord for discernment and don't be afraid to ask your spouse questions about what you are observing in them.

You will see other signs of the fruit of repentance. There will be a renewed desire for the Word of God and prayer. S/he will begin to desire spiritual things again and their spiritual walk will deepen in a way that was never there before.

S/he will also desire a renewed relationship with you. With repentance comes sorrow for the damage s/he did to you as the marriage partner. Very often the offending spouse will state that their husband/wife did not deserve such treatment and they will endure a great deal of guilt and sorrow seeing how you are suffering because of their sin.

When true repentance has taken place, the offender will do just about anything to show you that they have repented. They are very willing to be transparent and to be held accountable for their time and money.

Sometimes repentance takes place before the spouse is even aware of the sin's existence. It can be a difficult blow to take when you learn that your husband/wife was involved in sexual sin unbeknownst to you. There are times that a spouse will make a confession as the last part of their repentance period, or even years or decades later because the Lord will allow them no rest until they do.

Repentance is a by-product of Christ's life in the believer. It is spurred on by the person of the Holy Spirit working in the regenerated heart (the immaterial man). Repentance is a result of gaining a glimpse of the Beautiful One and His love and sacrifice. It occurs when the sinner comes face-to-face with the price of the sin that is so casually committed and realizes the cost of atoning for it. It is a love response that is supernatural.

The Bible does not contain a divorce option or provision for a spouse who has repented of their sexual sin and now walks in righteousness. The husband or wife of the repentant person is to forgive the sin and remain in the marriage.

However, just because your spouse repents, everything is not "fixed." There are reasons a person commits sexual sin. Some of these reasons have to do with your marriage and relationship; others have nothing to do with you at all.

You and your spouse have to uncover, discover, and work through the underlying issues in your relationship to strengthen it and to ward off sexual sin in the future. If you don't do these things, it is like putting a Band-Aid on a gaping wound.

While repentance is permanent when genuine, it still takes constant diligence. The repentant person can never look casually at sin and think s/he is somehow above it. Anytime the heart returns to a prideful place of exalting self, new areas of repentance need to be undertaken. Sanctification is a lifelong act.

CHAPTER 11
The Unrepentant

Before going forward with how you can live with an unrepentant spouse, I want you to know that whether s/he repents of their sexual sin or not, you can choose to stay with him/her. There is no law that says you should only stay with your spouse if s/he repents.

Frankly, the ugly truth is that many Christian marriages have at least one spouse who is involved with sexual sin through pornography. A whopping 53% of men who responded to a survey[22] said that they viewed pornography within one week of attending a Promise Keeper's event, and this same survey says that pornography is "a major problem" in 47% of Christian homes. With statistics like these, it is very safe to say that easily half of our Christian homes fit the profile I am addressing here: half of you reading this book are in a marriage where one of you is involved in unrepentant sexual sin with pornography. In many cases, one spouse is completely unaware that the other views pornography, especially if it is the wife who is accessing the porn. 70% of women who access porn keep it a secret.[23]

Obviously, it is much easier to live with someone who is committing sexual sin of which you are not aware. When the sin is exposed and your husband/wife is caught or admits they are watching pornography or has a lover (physical or emotional), things can take a very sharp turn for the worse, but there is also something akin to relief that is described by husbands and wives who learn the truth. While there is no comfort in the knowledge of infidelity, there is consolation to the spouse in finally knowing they are not crazy or imagining things.

However, having this information does not make things "better." In fact, the more you know the more difficult it can be to honor God in the relationship, but it can be done when you rely on Christ.

Living with the day-to-day reality that your spouse is a sexual sinner is a heavy burden to bear. The grief and sorrow can at times feel overwhelming and this is a very lonely way to live.

Because sexual sin is considered so shameful in the church, few people are willing to discuss it in settings where both the sexual sinner and his/her spouse can get help and support. Many couples fear others knowing the reality of their situation. Fear of the spouse being judged as some sort of "super sinner" or pervert is a common concern I hear. There is also fear of what others may think and s/he never repents and stops the sinful behavior.

There is something you will have to accept if you are going to stay and fight for your marriage: you cannot change your spouse, only God can. You will have to come to terms with the reality that you are not in control of any aspect of this marriage and that you cannot prevent him/her from continuing in sexual sin. Those who live with a man/woman who refuses to repent are encouraged to consistently pray for them, asking the Lord to give them the gift of repentance.

I previously addressed[24] the issue of how to deal with a spouse who views pornography, so I will not go into those specifics here. However, sexual sin is not only pornography and the ability to remain in a marriage with someone who is involved with it requires a tremendous commitment to the Lord.

The heartache of being sinned against

There is incredible heartache involved when a man/woman remains in a marriage like this. You will experience *much* heartache, *much* sorrow, *much* loneliness, and possibly take *much* abuse from your husband/wife while s/he is living in sexual sin—particularly as you continue to grow and change in your relationship with Christ.

Your transformation into Christ-likeness will most likely eat away at your spouse internally. They know they are deserving of your wrath and hatred and they will most likely not understand why you don't leave them or divorce them. S/he may tell you that if they were in your shoes, they would have already been gone or filed for divorce. Some spouses are cruel and will actually taunt their husband/wife for wanting to remain married in spite of the sexual sin.

If you refuse to respond in kind, this may cause the sinning spouse to experience great guilt at how s/he is treating you. The more you maintain the side of righteousness, the harder it will be for him/her to be near you because you remind him/her too much of Christ.

The sinning spouse may avoid you entirely, coming and going when they know you are not there. S/he may only communicate via text message or email to avoid seeing you. May I encourage you by telling you that such treatment is evidence that you are honoring God.

Sinners want others to join them in sin and will often accuse the husband/wife who desires to live a holy life of being pompous, pious, or "holier than thou." Do not be surprised by this for those involved in darkness are offended when Christians refuse to join in.

> *Therefore, since Christ has suffered in the flesh, arm yourselves also with the same purpose, because He who has suffered in the flesh has ceased from sin, so as to live the rest of the time in the flesh no longer for the lusts of men, but for the will of God. For the time already past is sufficient for you to have carried out the desire of the Gentiles, having pursued a course of sensuality, lusts, drunkenness, carousing, drinking parties and abominable idolatries. In all this, they are surprised that you do not run with them into the same excesses of dissipation, and they malign you; but they will give account to Him who is ready to judge the living and the dead. For the gospel has for this purpose been preached even to those who are dead, that though they are judged in the flesh as men, they may live in the spirit according to the will of God.* 1 Peter 4:1—6

Hope in heartache

Peter wrote two epistles to encourage the persecuted churches who were suffering horrifically because of Nero.

John MacArthur writes in the Introduction to the first epistle:

> Since the believers addressed were suffering escalating persecution, the purpose of this letter was to teach them how to live victoriously in the midst of that hostility: 1) without losing hope; 2) without becoming bitter; 3) while trusting in their Lord; and 4) while looking for His second coming. Peter wished to impress on his readers that by living an obedient, victorious life under duress, a Christian can actually evangelize his hostile world.[25]

The more you are like Christ in your marriage, the more persecution you may endure. Take seriously the four purposes for which Peter wrote these letters that you might follow his instruction and admonition.

The second greatest adversary you may face in this fight are your feelings.

> *Dear friends, as resident aliens and refugees, I urge you to keep at a safe distance from the fleshly desires that are poised against your soul like an expeditionary force, having good behavior among the Gentiles, so that while they slander you as wrongdoers, by observing your fine deeds they may glorify God on the day of inspection.*
>
> 1 Peter 2:11—12 (CCNT)

In this passage, Peter personifies feelings (fleshly desires) as though they were predatory and on the hunt with intent to capture and destroy the Christian.

Peter is saying that feelings have a way of wanting to take over your life if you let them. Our fleshly desires are lusty (Galatians 5:19-21). We must be alert to their wiles and learn to order our steps by the Word and the Spirit. It is very easy to become undisciplined and to allow our feelings to dictate our actions instead of letting the Word and the Spirit of God order our steps.

If you are a feelings-oriented person, you may have a hard time persevering this way because your feelings may discourage you to the point of giving up or giving in to sin.

Suffering is difficult, and suffering for doing what is right is somehow harder than suffering for doing what is wrong. Our Lord knows this and again we look to Peter's first epistle for encouragement:

> *Servants, be submissive to your masters with all respect, not only to those who are good and gentil, but also to those who are unreasonable (or perverse). For this finds favor, if for the sake of conscience toward God a person bears up under sorrows when suffering unjustly. For what credit is there if, when you sin and are harshly treated, you endure it with patience? But if when you do what is right and suffer for it you patiently endure it, this finds favor with God.*

> *For you have been called for this purpose, since Christ also suffered for you, leaving you an example for you to follow in His steps, WHO COMMITTED NO SIN, NOR WAS ANY DECEIT FOUND IN HIS MOUTH; and while being reviled, He did not revile in return; while suffering, He uttered no threats, but kept entrusting Himself to Him who judges righteously.*
>
> 1 Peter 2:18—23

While this passage was written for slaves who had ungodly owners, we can make application to situations where we are under the authority of someone who treats us harshly. In this case, it would be when the unrepentant spouse is hostile toward you because you are showing them love, forgiving them, and wanting to make your marriage work.

Your example is that of Christ Jesus who, as the Scripture says, did not retaliate or revile in return when He was persecuted, but entrusted Himself to God. Like Jesus, you can hand yourself over to the Lord to avenge and vindicate you (Romans 12:17—21). You do not need to repay evil for evil, but trust the Lord to take care of you.

Notice this passage also reminds us that we receive grace when we suffer unjustly, especially when doing good things for another person. God will give you the ability to endure the pain and suffering; He promises to do this.

Some of your friends and loved ones won't understand what you are doing. They will encourage you to fight back, get a divorce, or they will just say you are plain crazy to tolerate such behavior from your spouse. Frankly, *you* may wonder about the wisdom of your commitment because of the intensity of the pain you will endure.

Because there may be times you simply need encouragement, I want to direct you to 1 Peter 3: 13—17. Here Peter again reminds us that we are blessed when we suffer for doing what is good. He also says that the person suffering righteously is a powerful witness for God.

> *Who is there to harm you if you prove zealous for what is good? But even if you should suffer for the sake of righteousness, you are blessed. And do not fear their intimidation, and do not be troubled, but sanctify Christ as Lord in your hearts, always being ready to make a defense to everyone who asks you to give an account for the hope that is in you, yet with gentleness and reverence; and keep a good conscience so that in the thing in which you are slandered, those who revile your good behavior in Christ will be put to shame. For it is better, if God should will it so, that you suffer for doing what is right rather than for doing what is wrong.*
>
> 1 Peter 3:13—17

Determining to stay with your unrepentant spouse is not the easiest decision you will ever make, but the Lord will use it in your life and in the lives of those you encounter as you give testimony to His goodness and faithfulness to you in your suffering. The person you may have the most effect on is your husband/wife and it may be the means by which they repent.

I want to caution you though that there are no guarantees that your spouse will certainly repent as a result of your suffering for righteousness' sake. Your motive cannot be a form of martyrdom. Neither can it be to wallow in self-pity or to gain the attention and favor of others. If you choose to live with a spouse who is unrepentant of sexual sin, the only honorable motive is to glorify God.

Both 1 and 2 Peter are rich fertile ground for the soul of the suffering saint. I highly recommend you spend time reading and meditating on these two books of the Bible.

The Divorce Option

> But I say to you that everyone who divorces his wife, except on the ground of sexual immorality, makes her commit adultery, and whoever marries a divorced woman commits adultery.
> Matthew 5:32 (ESV)

One of the first questions a hurt and angry spouse who has learned of their husband/wife's sexual immorality will ask is if they can get a divorce. The emotions are running high and typically they are not thinking biblically or even rationally. The heat of those first several days is not the time to make a decision that will affect the rest of your life and the lives of your children. I truly believe that by God's grace and with His help your marriage can survive even this.

You will have many people telling you what they think or feel you ought to do, or what they did or would do themselves if they were in your shoes. Some of them mean well and sincerely want to help you deal with this trauma; others will attempt to relive their own experience through yours.

Some general guidelines you may find helpful are these:

- Accept counsel only from Bible believing Christians. While others in your life will want to help you, unless they are Christians who believe God's Word is infallible and accept it as their final authority their counsel will not agree with the counsel you would receive from someone who believes those things.

- Require those who give you advice to back it up with Scripture and then take the time to research it to be sure it is correctly used and in context.

- Find a good Biblical Counselor who will help you to see this problem from God's perspective. You need an objective source to help you discern what is true and what is false, right and wrong. Because your emotions are running high you may tend to react in anger and with a vengeful mindset.

Yes, your spouse has sinned grievously before God and you. Yes, according to Matthew 5:32, sexual immorality (porneia) is an acceptable reason for a divorce, but you must understand that God hates divorce (Malachi 2:14–16). Of course, God also hates the sexual immorality that has brought the topic of divorce to the forefront of your mind right now. Your marriage was designed to be one flesh for your entire life and the sin that has been committed has obliterated everything the Bible says marriage is supposed to be.

Divorce is allowed, but the Scripture says it was not a part of God's original plan for marriage. Divorce is allowed because of the "hardness of man's heart" (Matthew 19:8). While divorce is an option, it should be the very last thing on the list of considerations for you.

Elsewhere in this book[26] I have discussed the Marriage Covenant and how God intends for it to be permanent. Divorce is a concession that God allows when sexual sin has occurred or when a spouse is abandoned (Matthew 5:32, 19:9; 1 Corinthians 7:12–15). I have had cases where a spouse wants to hold onto the covenant that was made as reason *not* to divorce, but you must remember that when sexual sin takes place, the sinning party violates what they vowed to do. The covenant is broken and is no longer in force. It is admirable to want to remain married, and of course it is the goal of counseling—but clinging to a broken covenant is not the ground to make a stand.[27]

It is vital that before any divorce proceedings take place, the process of church discipline be allowed to run its course. 1 Corinthians 6:1–6 makes it clear that "outsiders" (i.e. civil courts) must not be involved

> Even though my husband won't talk to me and has moved out and told me he will be divorcing me I still have hope he will repent. I pray daily that God would work in his heart and continue to show him love and compassion when I have the chance to do so. I invite him to our home, invite him to family events, give him gifts and cards that remind him I am still his wife and still love him. I want him to come home.
>
> ~Josie, wife of Jose

in the business between church members prior to the church "ruling" on the matter. In other words, a church must determine through the Matthew 18 process if a refusal to repent will leave the church leadership no alternative than to declare a member as an unbeliever and a heathen. This excommunication places him or her outside the church which will free the remaining (believing) partner to pursue divorce if s/he desires (1 Corinthians 7:10—16).

The goal in every circumstance is reconciliation. This is why divorce must be the absolute last resort. Unfortunately, many churches do not practice the principles found in Matthew 18, considering them to be harsh or unloving and preferring to adopt a wait and see attitude toward sin of this magnitude.

There are cases when the husband/wife who is involved in adultery will actually leave or abandon their spouse for another man or woman. This is considered desertion and is also grounds for a divorce in the eyes of most churches. Abandonment places a person in a very difficult position financially and practically. Virtually every aspect of life is affected when one partner in a marriage leaves the other, and there are times that the civil authorities must be involved prior to the church leadership completing the discipline and restoration process.

This is why solid biblical counseling from church leadership or from lay counselors is imperative. A man who is unrepentant and leaves his wife for another woman and is unwilling to file for divorce after a long period of time is stringing her along for his own purposes. The abandoned spouse will need counsel as to how to proceed. Many churches are aware of litigators who are Bible believing Christians and will help a spouse navigate through a divorce in a manner that will uphold their Christian convictions even in the midst of such ungodly circumstances.

Divorce should always be the last option. The Lord desires we work toward reconciliation and forgiveness. It is certainly the example Jesus gave us. You don't have to divorce your spouse even if they refuse to repent!

As long as you are a positive influence in their life there is a chance they might repent. I believe this is at the heart of what Peter was teaching both men and women in 1 Peter 3 when he is speaking of wives submitting to and possibly winning their husbands without a word (1 Peter 3:1—6) and when he commanded husbands to live with their wives in an understanding way (1 Peter 3: 7) and to pray for them.[28]

CHAPTER 12

Between You and Him Alone

Matthew 18:15

If your brother sins, go and show him his fault in private; if he listens to you, you have won your brother. Matthew 18:15

Some spouses choose to stay in the marriage and try to win their husband/wife back. Living with a spouse who you know is actively engaging in sexual sin is very, very difficult, but it can be done. The majority of women whose husbands are involved in pornography choose to stay in their marriage.

It is critical to note that the Bible allows divorce in cases where the marriage covenant has been broken. Where there is ongoing unrepentant sexual sin (pornea), including adultery, homosexuality, bestiality and incest, divorce is allowed when all other options have been exhausted. According to Matthew 5:32 and 1 Corinthians 7:15, the faithful spouse can choose to divorce their husband or wife providing they have made *every effort* to bring the sinning partner back to repentance. This includes the involvement of the church, counseling, and after church discipline and biblical counseling. If the offender remains unrepentant, there may be no other alternative.

It must be said that there is no direct or specific divorce provision when a spouse is unrepentant for viewing pornography. Matthew 5:27 is clear that a man commits adultery in his heart when he looks lustfully at a woman. A person can lust while watching commercials on television, driving down the highway and seeing a billboard, or having a lingerie magazine arrive at home.

Jesus is saying in Matthew 5:27 that a man (or woman) who looks on another person lustfully has committed adultery with that person in his or her heart. This is a critical point that demands explanation so as to be understood correctly. The Greek word for "looks" means a continuous, repeated action. He says that if you are looking with the purpose and intent of lusting after another person you have already committed the adultery in your heart. (Looking was the caboose on the train.) Looking was the result, the fruit of what was already happening in the inner man.

John MacArthur, in a sermon on adultery, says this:

> The heart is filled with adultery, wanting to find an object to which to attach the fantasy. It's when . . . you're looking for the woman to lust after, when you . . . go to the film because you know when you get there you will see what you desire in your heart to see, that which will meet your lust. It's when you go around the dial on the television to find the thing that panders your lust. It's when you seek the object, it's the purpose. So it would read this way: "emphatically I say to you that whoever continues looking on a woman for the purpose of lusting gives evidence of already committing adultery in his heart." The continued look is the manifestation of the vile heart. The aorist infinitive here is an accomplished lusting; you've already done it, you've filled it up, this is just the last element. It's already done. [29]

This is a very difficult area to address. Emotions run very high when dealing with pornography and there is no consensus in the church on the matter. More liberal churches will not consider pornography to be adultery, and the more conservative churches will consider it so. Pornography as "adultery" that makes divorce legitimate seems to be an issue churches are willing to flex on.

Biblically speaking, the lust of the heart is the root of the problem; therefore, the heart must ultimately be addressed with respect to repentance. Due to this we have to examine the role of the church in cases of known sexual sin.

Paul severely rebuked the Corinthian church for their tolerance of sexual immorality:

> *It is actually reported that there is immorality among you, and immorality of such a kind as does not exist even among the*

126

Gentiles, that someone has his father's wife. You have become arrogant and have not mourned instead, so that the one who had done this deed would be removed from your midst.

For I, on my part, though absent in body but present in spirit, have already judged him who has so committed this, as though I were present. In the name of our Lord Jesus, when you are assembled, and I with you in spirit, with the power of our Lord Jesus, I have decided to deliver such a one to Satan for the destruction of his flesh, so that his spirit may be saved in the day of the Lord Jesus.

Your boasting is not good. Do you not know that a little leaven leavens the whole lump of dough? Clean out the old leaven so that you may be a new lump, just as you are in fact unleavened. For Christ our Passover also has been sacrificed. Therefore let us celebrate the feast, not with old leaven, nor with the leaven of malice and wickedness, but with the unleavened bread of sincerity and truth.

I wrote you in my letter not to associate with immoral people; I did not at all mean with the immoral people of this world, or with the covetous and swindlers, or with idolaters, for then you would have to go out of the world. But actually, I wrote to you not to associate with any so-called brother if he is an immoral person, or covetous, or an idolater, or a reviler, or a drunkard, or a swindler—not even to eat with such a one. For what have I to do with judging outsiders? Do you not judge those who are within the church? But those who are outside, God judges. REMOVE THE WICKED MAN FROM AMONG YOURSELVES. 1 Corinthians 5:1—13

The words are clear: the Church is not to tolerate sexual immorality among her members. This means that when a spouse learns their husband/wife is sexually immoral, the church leadership is to be informed.

It is always better if the man/woman is willing to go voluntarily and confess their sin and ask for help. That is demonstration of an aspect of true repentance, and allows the church to surround him/her with love, compassion, and accountability. When the church is allowed to teach, rebuke, correct, and train in righteousness (1 Timothy 3:16) everyone is better off! The individual repents and continues to grow and change, the church is purified and the body is protected. Unfortunately, this is rarer than I like it to be.

The usual course of action is quite the opposite. Sin hates exposure and so the man/woman involved in sexual sin is often desperate to keep things hidden and secret. Regardless of personal feelings on the matter, the prescribed process must be followed to assist the person in repentance and change. This is for their good and God's glory.

In the Gospel of Matthew we find the passage on what is commonly called "church discipline." Personally, I think it is a terrible way to refer to such a loving and gracious process. This passage is certainly corrective, but it is also restorative and intended to bring the wandering sheep back to the fold.

> *What do you think? If any man has a hundred sheep, and one of them has gone astray, does he not leave the ninety-nine on the mountains and go and search for the one that is straying? If it turns out that he finds it, truly I say to you, he rejoices over it more than over the ninety-nine which have not gone astray. So it is not the will of your Father who is in heaven that one of these little ones perish.*
>
> *If your brother sins, go and show him his fault in private; if he listens to you, you have won your brother. But if he does not listen to you, take one or two more with you, so that BY THE MOUTH OF TWO OR THREE WITNESSES EVERY FACT MAY BE CONFIRMED. If he refuses to listen to them, tell it to the church; and if he refuses to listen even to the church, let him be to you as a Gentile and a tax collector.*
>
> Matthew 18: 12—17

There have been many books written on the process of discipline and restoration so I shall not belabor the matter here in great detail. I do think it will be helpful for our purposes to look at this important text and how it applies in responding to sexual immorality.

In a previous section of this book[30], I outlined true biblical repentance. I wrote that a person who is a Christian *will* repent of their sin because they will not be able to withstand the pressure, pain, and misery that the Holy Spirit will bring into their life. Very often it is the process of Matthew 18 that aids in helping a person to repent.

When a husband or wife learns that their spouse has been sinning sexually, the first response is to confront them. Unfortunately, the first interaction between the spouses is often volatile and hostile, traumatic and full of tears and sorrow. It is very difficult to approach sexual sin objectively because it is so *hurtful* to the spouse who learns of it.

Matthew 18:15 tells us to confront a sinning brother or sister alone or in private.

This is the first step of the process. It is so important to be certain that what is being confronted is actually *sin*. There should be evidence of the sin or strong suspicion of the sin that is followed up by heart level questions that are aimed at exposing the heart of truth.

Evidence would include things like: pop-up pornography on the computer, computer history log with pornography websites, finding magazines or movies, missing money, missing time in the day, being "nowhere" for extended periods of time, finding receipts from places you have not been with your spouse, text messages, emails, love letters, mysterious phone calls, finding a secret cell phone or credit card, and other concrete things like these.

I consider strong suspicion to be having bits and pieces of information that makes you wonder, but not enough concrete evidence to make an accusation.

I do not recommend making accusations, even with evidence in hand. Questions are a better way to learn truth because heart level questions will often prick the conscience of the hearer. Questions such as those that follow are intended to cause or lead the person to admit their sin.

- Would you please tell me about this receipt I found?
- Can you tell me about the pornography I found on the computer?
- What do you know about this charge on our credit card?
- I noticed some text messages on your phone, will you tell me about them?
- Will you talk to me about where you have been tonight?
- I am concerned about some things I have learned today, can we talk about them?
- I found pornography in your briefcase; will you tell me how long this has been a problem for you?
- I was sent a text message/email by someone today, would you tell me what has been going on with you and (name)?

You may think that such a response is not realistic, but by prayer and the power of the Holy Spirit ruling in your heart in those moments, they can be!

As your husband/wife answers your questions, you will want to continue to narrow the scope of any further questions you have until your spouse either admits their sin or refuses to discuss it further. If s/he refuses to discuss it anymore let him/her know that you will give them some time to think about the issue, but that it is not a closed conversation. If your evidence is strong, you may consider asking him/her outright if your suspicions are true.

We will walk through the story of Randy and Sandra to illustrate the process. This couple has been married for 17 years. Sandra returned home from visiting out of town family and while preparing to do the laundry she found several receipts in Randy's pocket that caused alarm.

Rather than flying off the handle, she attempted to determine if these receipts were work-related or whether they might explain the changes she noticed in her husband over the past several months. He had become distant and quiet, preferring to spend time alone instead of with Sandra. He was frequently sleepless and restless; this led to a bad temper and he was easily provoked to anger with her.

Their intimacy had fallen off during this time too, but Sandra wanted to attribute it to work related stress which she knew Randy was experiencing.

When Sandra found the receipts she checked the bank account and noticed that Randy had made several withdrawals from their savings account the day before the date on the receipts. She remembered that he told her he was going out for a while to run some errands and declined her offer to accompany him.

Sandra then searched the computer to see if there was anything she could find in the way of emails, instant messages, or social networking contacts that would confirm or debunk her growing suspicions. She checked the cell phone records and saw an abundance of contacts in the form of calls and text messages from her husband's number to a number she did not recognize. When Sandra called the number she got the voice mail for a woman named "Molly."

Sandra declined to leave a message, but used reverse number look up on the internet to see if she could find any information on Molly, hoping to dispel her growing suspicions and the sickening feeling in her stomach.

She learned that Molly lived about 10 miles away from them, her age, and her address. She planned to confront Randy when he came home from work that night. She spent time in prayer, asking the Lord to reveal the truth to her and praying she would not do something sinful that would do more damage to her marriage.

> The day I learned that Randy had been unfaithful to me was the worst day of my life. When he came home from work I confronted him with the evidence I had that he had been with Molly while I was gone. I showed him the receipts I had found, and then the phone logs that had

> dozens and dozens of times their numbers were linked in text messages and phone calls. I asked him if he was having an affair with her. I told him that before he answered me, I wanted him to know that no matter what the answer was I was ready to hear it. I had wondered for so long what was wrong with him, and I wondered if it could be something like this, but honestly I never thought it would be!
>
> He denied it, and had all sorts of explanations about the receipts, the withdrawal of money, and the phone calls. I kept asking him questions about the timeline and the receipts; but he continued to deny everything.

Sandra followed the first step of the process: she confronted her husband privately. She asked him questions to attempt to verify the information she had and the suspicions that information raised. He repeatedly denied being involved in adultery and became angry at her questions.

Sandra continued to watch and pray over the days that followed. She checked the cell phone record at the next billing date and saw there were more exchanges between Molly and her husband.

> When I saw the cell phone bill had more phone and text contact between Molly and Randy I prepared to confront him again. The times of some of the calls were after work hours, when he would have been driving home or out doing errands and the texts were more during the day and on weekends.
>
> This time when I asked Randy about the phone logs I told him about the timing of the phone calls and text messages. I asked him to please just be honest with me, that I only wanted to know the truth! I told him I loved him and that I wanted to work things out. I asked him if he was being unfaithful to me, and again he denied it. This time he became very angry, storming around the house and yelling about how terrible I was to be accusing him of such a horrible thing. He told me that he

works hard so I can stay home and that I was very ungrateful for all he does for me. He said I was paranoid and I needed to knock it off because these accusations made me seem crazy.

She confronted Randy lovingly several more times over the following months and he consistently denied infidelity. The questions and denials caused additional strain between Sandra and Randy. He became more sullen and angry and she became more suspicious.

When Molly's phone number stopped showing up on our phone bill I thought maybe it was over. There continued to be small withdrawals of cash from the bank that he always seemed to be able to explain. He had to take a client for coffee, he needed a part for the lawnmower, or he wanted a burger instead of the lunch he took to work that day, those kinds of things.

I don't know what made me finally give in to the urge to drive past her house. I had been resisting for so long, telling myself that I was just being silly. I think part of me was really afraid of what I might see, and what I might learn.

The day I went to her house I thought I would just drive by. Randy was at a meeting in the city and would not be back until late that night because the meeting was with an important client. He had been preparing for weeks for this meeting so I was sure it was true.

I found her house with relative ease and drove slowly down the block watching the addresses to be sure I didn't miss it or was not being obvious. All I needed was to get a ticket for stalking or something! Her house looked like all the others, nice and neat, well cared for on the outside. I remember seeing lots of flowers and thought of how my own gardens were such a matter of contention between Randy and me. He hated having to weed them and all the work that the flower beds required all spring and summer.

Nothing looked out of order, no cars in the driveway and no signs of life. As I drove past the house feeling perfectly silly for being suspicious and very guilty, I saw movement in the rear view mirror. I saw two people on the deck on the back of the house who were locked in a passionate embrace. The woman was a little overweight and blonde and the man was my husband.

I don't recall driving home but I know I got there. I spent the rest of the day trying to figure out what I was going to say or do when Randy came home. I honestly thought about assaulting him. I thought about going back and confronting them together; I thought about packing up and leaving. I know I cried a lot.

When Randy came home I asked him how his day had been. I asked him how his meeting with that "important client" went and if all his hard prep work had paid off. He told me the meeting went very well, but that he suspected he would be having additional meetings with that client and possibly an out of town trip associated with it as well.

I have no idea how I kept it together other than the grace of God because I knew he was lying right to my face. I began to ask him questions about the place the meeting was held, what he ate, who the speakers were, who was there with him, that sort of thing.

I was careful not to make it like an inquisition, but more like his wife who wanted to be involved in his world. Randy quickly became frustrated with me because he was clearly not prepared to answer my friendly questions.

Finally I just looked at him and told him I knew where he was that day. He stammered out something about having been at that meeting and that I was being ridiculous. I took a big breath and said, "I drove past her house today and I saw you kissing on the deck."

All the blood drained out of his face and I honestly thought he might faint. He tried to keep up with the lies, but he knew that I knew and after a few minutes he slumped against the counter and put his face in his hands. He would not talk to me about anything, no matter how I asked him to talk about it. He left the room without a word.

CHAPTER 13
The Role of the Church
Matthew 18:16—20

But if he does not listen to you, take one or two more with you, so that BY THE MOUTH OF TWO OR THREE WITNESSES EVERY FACT MAY BE CONFIRMED. If he refuses to listen to them, tell it to the church; and if he refuses to listen even to the church, let him be to you as a gentile and a tax collector. Truly I say to you, whatever you bind on earth shall have been bound in heaven; and whatever you loose on earth shall have been loosed in heaven. Again I say to you, that if two of you agree on earth about anything that they may ask, it shall be done for them by My Father who is in heaven. For where two or three have gathered together in My name, I am there in their midst.

Matthew 18:16-20

The Church has a huge role to play in cases of unrepentant sexual sins. There are actions the church *must* take and we will look at those in this chapter through the continued example of Randy and Sandra.

The next day Sandra went to the church and told her Pastor everything she knew. The Pastor, Dan, told her that over the past several months he could tell something was wrong with Randy, and had hoped that infidelity was not in play. Pastor Dan patiently explained to her that Randy must be confronted about his sin and called to repentance. Because Randy had been unwilling to talk to Sandra about anything, it was difficult to discern what he was thinking or if he had any plans to leave or divorce Sandra.

The plan was made to continue the process of discipline with Randy. Pastor Dan instructed Sandra to pray specifically that Randy would repent of his sin. She was also to urge Randy to talk about the matter, to break the relationship off, and to ask him questions about what he was planning to do with their marriage.

Despite Sandra's knowledge of his sin, Randy continued to live in the home with her. This was very painful and difficult for Sandra; her whole life was coming apart and there were many times each day when she was tempted to rage at Randy when he was home. He was unwilling to talk with her about the other woman and Sandra knew he continued to see her whenever he could.

> I struggled so much; every hour of the day was heartache. Randy stopped taking my calls and let them all go to voicemail. If I would text him about something not related to us or our marriage he might reply, but if I sent him an "I love you" message he would not respond at all. I didn't know what happened to the man I married. He started sleeping in the basement and coming and going whenever he pleased.
>
> I quickly learned that badgering him about Molly was unwise. There were times I said cruel things about her and him and that only served to push him further away from me.
>
> Pastor Dan asked me to take my hurt and pain to God, and to look at what Randy was doing from His perspective. He asked me if I knew what could have driven Randy to this woman, had there been trouble or fighting at home? I knew that we had gotten distant from each other, but I thought I was a good wife. I never thought anything like this would happen to me.

Sandra continued to ask Randy to repent and break off the relationship over the next several weeks and Randy responded with anger or indifference to any request Sandra had made. He stopped attending church and was seldom home on Sunday mornings. Sandra assumed he was sleeping at Molly's house.

Upon hearing Sandra's discouraging report, Pastor Dan asked Sandra to take a day to fast and pray for her marriage. While she was praying she was to ask the Lord what areas of failure in the marriage could she claim as her own? He asked her to make a list of all the sin she could think of that she had committed against Randy and then confess it to God. Once she dealt with her sin before God she was to ask Randy if he would sit and listen to her make a confession to him and ask his forgiveness for her failings in their marriage.

When there is marital discord, there is usually much sin that has been swept under the rug throughout many years. Issues that were never dealt with, anger that has festered, and deeply rooted bitterness in the hearts of both husband and wife only need a spark to set off a firestorm of adultery.

A proverbial clearing of the deck is needed in the relationship if there is any hope of restoration. At least one marriage partner has to humble themselves and confess the sin they have harbored for so long.

This was very humbling for me to do, and while I was fine with confessing my sins to God, I was not at all interested in confessing my sins to Randy, the guy who was cheating on me! I was so angry that I had to ask him to forgive me when he was the one cheating! It just didn't make sense to me, but Pastor Dan told me that if the Matthew 18 process was to have any chance at success I had to get the logs out of my own eye (Matthew 7). Because I really wanted to do what was right and get my husband back I agreed to do it.

It took me several days to write out all that I knew I had done against Randy over the many years of our marriage. I asked Pastor Dan to look over my list to see if it seemed right and then I planned how I was going to get Randy to stay and listen to me.

I waited until he came home from being out on a Friday night. I was in the bedroom and when I heard him come in and head down to the basement where he was now sleeping. I prayed, gathered my courage and went down to talk to him. He was getting ready for bed, and he was not glad to see me.

I asked him if I could please talk to him for a few minutes and told him I was not going to say anything bad about him or her, but that I had some things I needed to say and ask him.

He rolled his eyes and gave a loud sigh and sat down on the edge of the bed. I began by telling him that I was still praying for him to repent and he immediately got up and started yelling that he just knew I could not be trusted and that he should have not bothered to come home. He told me he didn't want to be badgered and that he didn't want to hear anything I had to say.

I told him that I was not going to badger him, but I did have some things I needed to tell him and I asked him again to sit and listen. I was so thankful he agreed. I began by telling him that I know I was not the best wife and that the Lord had been showing me some things about myself over the past months. I started reading my list of "logs" and asked him to forgive me for sinning and not being a very good wife to him.

He waited until I was through and asked me if that was it, was that all I had to say? When I asked him if he forgave me he told me he did, but that it was not going to change anything. It was too late, he said. He was in love with Molly and planned to leave me as soon as he could get everything in place.

It was like I was punched in the stomach. I could not breathe, I could not cry. I just stood there, looking at him...astonished I guess at what I thought I heard him say. I could not believe my husband had just told me he loved another woman. It did not make one bit of sense.

I did not understand; I had done what the Pastor asked me to do! Why could he not understand that I loved and needed him? Had I been *that* horrible?

When I told Pastor Dan what Randy's response had been, he told me that it was time to change things. He told me that I had been patient with Randy and that I had gone to him many times over the past several months with no sign of repentance, so it was time to get someone else involved.

But if he does not listen to you, take one or two more with you, so that BY THE MOUTH OF TWO OR THREE WITNESSES EVERY FACT MAY BE CONFIRMED.　　　Matthew 18:16

Pastor Dan explained to Sandra that when a person refuses to repent when urged to privately, the next step is to pray and ask the Lord which of the unrepentant person's friends or family members would be good choices to go with you in a small group confrontation.

It is very important that those who go to confront another person are spiritually mature believers, not prone to gossip or harshness. It is much more desirable to choose men or women who are winsome and will lovingly urge the unrepentant sinner towards conviction and forsaking of the sin in which they are caught up. It is helpful if there is already an established relationship between the individuals. Ideally, they should be people whom the unrepentant sinner respects.

Each person must be entrusted with enough details to be able to accurately discuss the matter at hand. Each must also commit to pray daily for the one they confront and be bold to speak the truth in love. Personal confrontation is necessary; however, it is unwise to hurry or "hit and run" such a conversation.

The unrepentant sinner must be asked to confirm the facts of the case. This is for accountability and follows the procedure God used in Genesis 3 when Adam sinned and he and Eve hid in the bushes. When the facts are out, the confronting person must ask the unrepentant sinner if s/he is willing to repent and forsake their sin. S/he must be reminded of the serious nature of sin and the sacrificial death of Christ that paid the penalty for sin. S/he must be reminded that this process could end in their being removed from church fellowship as a result of rebellion toward God and the authorities He has put in place in the church.

> *Therefore, confess your sins to one another, and pray for one another so that you may be healed. The effective prayer of a righteous man can accomplish much.* James 5:16

I chose two men who had been in Randy's life for many years. John and Bill both are godly men who are a little older than Randy. I trusted they would give him the truth that he needed to hear.

John met Randy for coffee over lunch one day and, according to John, Randy was furious that I had gotten him involved. He said Randy listened to everything he said and was willing to look at the Scriptures but was unwilling to commit to any course of action. According to John, Randy said he needed time. He was not willing to say how much time or why he needed time, just that he did. The meeting ended with Randy telling John he would call him soon.

When Randy came home after work that night he gave me the cold, cold shoulder. He ignored me as he went to the basement to change and all he said to me when he came up was, "It won't work. I am not staying with you."

This stage, like the first one, can take weeks or even months. It is wise to allow sufficient time for the conscience to be affected by the Scriptural truth being presented by the small group of Christians who love the rebel enough to confront him/her with their sin. They must be fervent in prayer for him/her, interceding for them before God.

At each step in the process, Bill and John informed the Pastor what was said to Randy and what his response was to the rebuke and admonition to repent of his sexual sin. Pastor Dan guided each man through the Matthew 18 process, giving suggestions as to what additional Scriptures to use and how to biblically answer any objections Randy might have.

When Bill called Randy a few days later he must have figured what it was about right away because according to Bill, Randy asked him if I had put him up to it. Randy told Bill that there was no sense in wasting his time, that meeting would not change anything.

These were really discouraging events for me, because I really wanted Randy to repent! I continued to urge Randy to break it off with Molly and told him that I was still willing to do what I had to do to make it work. I told him I would go to counseling and everything, but he told me it would just be a waste of time.

John and Bill contacted Randy three or four more times and did manage to meet face-to-face at least once more each, but Randy was not willing to act on anything they said to him. He was getting more and more angry and hateful towards me and soon after the last meeting with Bill he told me he was moving out.

Pastor Dan also placed a call to Randy at least once a week. Unfortunately, his calls went unanswered. He did not return any messages that Pastor Dan left him. He had stopped coming to church months before and the only thing left was to try to meet Randy coming or going from work or home, or at Molly's house.

Pastor Dan and another Elder attempted to meet with Randy several times but were unable to connect with him, despite their efforts. When Randy announced he was moving out, the church had no option but to move to the third phase of the process.

> *If he refuses to listen to them, tell it to the church; and if he refuses to listen even to the church, let him be to you as a gentile and a tax collector.* Matthew 18: 17

When Randy moved out I felt like I was being ripped in half. He took as much stuff as he could pack in plastic bins and carried them one by one out to his car. Part of me could not believe it was happening; I kept waiting to wake up from this horrible nightmare! In spite of all he had done in the past year, I still loved him and I wanted him and our marriage.

I sobbed and begged him not to go. I told him we could work it out, that I loved him and needed him. I told him that there was nothing we could not face together and that he was all I ever wanted. I told him she would not make him happy, that in time he would see what a mistake he was making and that I would be here, waiting.

His face was hard. He was just so unmoved by anything that I was saying! I could not believe this was the same man I married. After his car was packed he came back in and stood by the door. He told me that he was sorry that he hurt me this way, but that he had not been happy for a long time. He told me that it was not really all my fault; that he knew he had some responsibility in our marriage breaking down like it had.

He told me that he was probably going to file for divorce once he got settled down. He said that it didn't matter what the church thought about what he was doing.

He was still a Christian and did not believe God wanted him to live a miserable life. He was pretty sure God wanted him to be happy, and that he spent too many years doing what other people wanted him to do. He was doing this for him. He said I would be hearing from him about the house and splitting the bills and other financial things. He even said I could call him if something happened at the house and I needed him to fix something.

The only thing he told me not to do was to keep badgering him about God. He said he didn't want the church people bugging him and that I was not to allow that to continue because it would not change his mind, in fact if I didn't call them off it would seal his decision to divorce me.

Pastor Dan was grieved to hear Randy had actually moved out. His threat to divorce Sandra was viewed as the manipulation that it was and the church proceeded with the next step.

At a special meeting of the Elder Board, Pastor Dan laid out for the men everything that had been done with Randy and Sandra. He gave them the necessary details of Randy's adultery and Sandra's willingness to submit herself to the church in counseling.

Pastor discussed Bill and John's attempts to urge Randy to repent and that Randy had rebuffed every rebuke and exhortation he had been given to that point. He sorrowfully told them that Randy had moved out and told Sandra he intended to divorce her.

After prayer for wisdom and carefully searching the Scriptures for the same, it was determined that telling the church of this situation was the next necessary step. They called a special meeting for church members after the Sunday Service.

The Elders stood together at the front of the church as Pastor Dan explained that a member of the church family had been in the process of Matthew 18 for many months. He gave the details that were needed: that Randy had been involved in adultery and had left home. Pastor Dan further said Randy intended to divorce Sandra. Sandra had been fully cooperative and wanted Randy to repent and come home. He asked the congregation to contact Randy and urge him to repent out of concern for his soul.

The pastor explained that while adultery was the sin that opened the process, the issue was now one of a refusal to repent, which is indicative of an unbeliever, not a regenerated Christian. He said that those willing to contact Randy should see the church secretary for Randy's contact information.

His careful instruction was that if a person chose to call or contact Randy, it was to be done with humility and love out of a deep concern for his heart and soul. There was not to be yelling or telling Randy he was a horrible person. There was to be no condemnation. Instead there should be rebuke born out of love and a sincere desire to see him restored to God, the church, and his wife. They were to let him know they were praying for him to repent of his sin and return to his wife and the church.

Pastor suggested that those who were going to contact him do so more than once, but not to be abusive or harassing. If Randy asked them not to call back, they were to respect his request.

Many people took up the challenge and contacted Randy through phone calls, mailing cards and letters. Several tried to meet with him personally, but were rebuffed. Despite the best efforts of the church, Randy was not responsive at all.

I had hoped that Randy would see the seriousness of the situation and repent. I was so encouraged to hear from so many people from church who tried to talk to him!

Randy became absolutely hateful toward me. Each time he was contacted by someone from church, he would call me screaming and swearing that I should tell them to back off and leave him alone. He told me that he was through with me and that he would be filing for divorce any day.

He stopped coming over when I needed him to fix something in the house, and after a few months, he was just silent. He would not respond to my calls or messages. I would drive past Molly's house sometimes and see his car in the driveway, so I knew he was still there.

I was so discouraged and so depressed. I could not imagine what I had done that was so wrong to cause him to hate me and to leave me the way he did. My church surrounded me with love and care during this whole ugly process.

In a second meeting of the church congregation, Pastor Dan, with the Elders, read Matthew 18:15-17 and recounted all the steps that had been taken with Randy over the past year. He thanked everyone who called and sent Randy cards and tried to confront him in love. He then read from 1 Corinthians 5:9—13, and with sorrow, said that Randy had been put out of the church "for the destruction of the flesh, that his spirit may be saved on the day of the Lord Jesus" (1 Corinthians 5:5 NKJV).

The final admonition Pastor Dan made was to ask the church body to keep Randy in prayer and to continue to urge repentance if presented with the opportunity.

In the narrative you just read, the leadership and the church followed the biblical pattern for discipline and restoration of a person who is unrepentant. The tragic thing is that not all, and in fact *most* Pastors/Elders do not practice any form of discipline in their churches other than to say, "Stop that!"

I am told by various leaders in ministry that there is a great amount of fear involved with this process because it makes the congregation unhappy, and those leaders believe the last thing they can afford to do is to make people unhappy. When people are unhappy or there is controversy, they demand meetings with the Pastor and leave the church. I say in love and with a great burden that far too often, upholding righteousness is forsaken for the almighty collection plate or for the false peace that is gained by ignoring sin.

A church is much healthier spiritually and in every other way when the members know that their leaders love them enough to address unrepentant sinful hearts. A healthy church has courageous leaders who do not fail to confront sin discreetly, compassionately and effectively.

Sandra was very blessed because her church family rallied around her in her time of need. They stuck close and encouraged her, helping to meet her practical and emotional needs when Randy would not. Again, this is part of the culture of a church that operates biblically.

Your experience may have been vastly different than Sandra's. You may believe that no one cares about you or your plight because there has been little or no compassion or help forthcoming for you or your unrepentant husband/wife. If this is the case, I urge you to sit down and talk with your church leadership and ask questions. It is possible that the leadership does not know how to help you! Be a part of the solution and determine to come alongside other people who are hurting and alone; determine to fulfill the command of Christ: love one another.

CHAPTER 14

Moving Forward: Together

The outcomes for the people whose stories went into this book have varied, and some are not yet finished being written. A few couples are still working on their marriages, and in other cases they have divorced for a variety of reasons.

The next several chapters address those who go forward together and those who do not. Each decision will have its own challenges and deserves its own attention to detail. Much of what is faced is beyond the scope of this book, and I urge you to seek or continue your biblical counseling relationship as you process through these changes in your life and marriage.

Together

We have looked at some very difficult things on this journey. I know at times it has been quite discouraging and hard to bear. I want you to know that there truly is hope after sexual sin in a marriage.

I have been a part of the lives of numerous couples who have put their marriages and families back together after weathering the storms brought about by sexual immorality.

You must understand that it will never be the same as it was before the sexual immorality took place. On its face, that statement may make you sad, but take a few moments and think about it. Do you really want that life back? You were married to a different person then, one who had secrets and was deceptive. Now things have been brought into the light and the Lord has revealed his/her heart. Hopefully, some changes have been made in both of you and you are able to be more honest and open with one another.

You *will* need counseling. Counsel separately, man to man and woman to woman, and then counsel as a couple with both counselors. The counselors should always be pointing you back toward the cross and restoration of the marriage relationship; pointing each of you in the direction of working on your own sinful thoughts, beliefs, and desires (Matthew 7:3–5).

The majority of our counseling cases involve two believers who say they are willing to submit to our counsel and say they are willing to change. What we find through the counseling process is that even when the initial issue of the sexual sin is dealt with biblically, there is much work yet to be done.

You will have to deal biblically with issues that are, in some cases, long-standing. You have to get at the roots of the problems that lead to the sexual sin. Each issue you bring to the counseling table should be looked at from a biblical perspective. The goal should be for each of you to individually determine to give God the glory by how you live your lives. This means confession and repentance must take place in each individual's heart.

You must determine to put God first in your lives followed by each other; everything and everyone falls in line after God and your spouse with very few exceptions.[31] Be careful not to idolize each other or your marriage in the process. A good biblical counselor can help you avoid that pitfall.

This process will be a *lot* of work and at times it may *feel* impossible and overwhelming to you. Remember in those moments (or days), that you did not get into this marital mess in one day and you most likely won't climb out of it quickly either.

It would be unrealistic and more importantly unbiblical to expect the hurting husband/wife to pretend or ignore the hurt and pain they endure. There has been betrayal; the faithful spouse has been wounded. S/he may be conflicted and have little inner peace due to the recurrent thoughts and memories. To pretend this inner conflict does not exist and to minimize its impact would be peace-faking[32] and, in reality, all that emotion would be driven underground to fester and become a cancerous spiritual issue. God has called us to live in peace and to address anger and other sin issues before the sun goes down (Ephesians 4:26, 27).

You, as the one who is hurting and struggling with the knowledge you possess, are responsible for getting help for the sin issues *you* are confronting in response to your husband/wife's former sexual sin. Reading this book is part of the process and I am thankful you are! It cannot stop here though; any change requires more than information. It requires action.

Intrusive Thoughts

When you choose to stay with your husband/wife, the pain of the offence does not go away, even when you forgive him or her. There will always be a scar on your heart. Like any deep wound that hit a nerve, it will be extra sensitive and prone to ache from time to time.

You may be more sensitive to television programs that discuss infidelity or sexual sin of any kind. One woman told me she no longer enjoyed weddings because she had this overwhelming urge to warn the bride that this happy day would not last, and she better be sure she protects her husband.

Because sexual sin is so deeply personal and intimate, you may find thoughts intruding into your everyday life at times you least expect them. You might find yourself sad at times for no apparent reason until you check your thoughts and understand that you are thinking on things of the past.

I am the definition of walking wounded. The pain I am living with is beyond description. I am thinking all the time about what I know of her sinful actions. I have *so* many ungodly thoughts about her sometimes; I want to tell her my thoughts about what she did to me in very worldly terms. I want her to know how much damage she did to me as a man and a husband. I know I have a harder time with intrusive thoughts at specific points in the day, and some days more than others. I am learning to refuse to meditate on those thoughts when they come into my head. I have to work on diverting them elsewhere. Then I thank God she came to her senses and is still with me and the kids.

~Heath

The world's way of addressing intrusive thoughts is to modify your behavior. Behavior modification is an ineffective way to lasting change. You must learn to do more than control your thinking; you must *change* your thinking. You must be renewed in your mind (Romans 12:2) through the Word of God.

The biblical method of changing your thinking begins in the heart and is a work of the Holy Spirit. Your growth and change in this area of your life will affect much more than your thoughts about your spouse's sexual sin and subsequent repentance; it will produce overall growth in Christ-likeness.

> *We destroy arguments and every lofty opinion raised against the knowledge of God, and take every thought captive to obey Christ.*　　　　　2 Corinthians 10:5 (ESV)

It is important to understand that we are not to allow our thoughts to have free reign. Scripture instructs us to take our thoughts captive (2 Corinthians 10:3–6), to fix our thoughts on God (Isaiah 26:3), and to be disciplined in our thinking (2 Timothy 1:7) as in other aspects of our lives.

You may not always be able to control whether thoughts of your husband/wife's sexual sins pop into your mind, but you *are* able to control what you do with those thoughts and how long they stay active. Past counselees have told me that when they meditated on the thoughts of their spouse's sexual sin they became harder to dislodge. It stands to reason, the more you play with any sin the greater the hold it has on you. The more you ruminate on the actions of the past the more the hurt stays alive, the betrayal feels fresh, and you remain stuck between the sin of the past and moving forward.

> I travel a lot for my job and it is a daily struggle to get into my car each morning to go to work. I am just so unsure of what he will be doing while I am gone! I walk into an invisible wall of fear each morning and it is all I can do to pull out of the driveway. I fight with myself all afternoon, wondering what is he doing, where is he now.

> I keep wondering if he has gone back to the (strip) club to see that girl while I am out working and can't watch over him.
>
> I know he said he has repented and that he hates his sin. I want to trust him but it is so hard to do so. I just don't know if it is real . . .
>
> ~Marcie, wife of Gordon

A man whose wife committed emotional adultery with an old high school friend she found on Facebook began to experience panic attacks at work. He worked nights and that was when his wife had been talking to the other man. He had witnessed his wife writing the private message to the man ending their relationship and telling him she was deleting the account, but he was very fearful she would create another one to keep in touch with the man.

In both of these cases and many others like them, the spouse who forgives experiences a kind of post-traumatic stress reaction when faced with the reality that their husband/wife could re-offend.

> Nan told me she repented and I do believe her...but I am scared. I am scared of not pleasing her and having her reach out to him again. I am scared I won't be enough for her, won't be a good enough friend to her or a good listener. I am afraid I won't please her sexually because I won't talk dirty to her like he did. I am scared all the time.
>
> ~Samuel, husband of Nan

The forgiving spouse can struggle with thoughts and memories that cause them to relive the trauma or re-experience the pain they felt when they learned of the immorality or infidelity. This struggle may exist even when it makes no sense for the former offender to be unfaithful again, and even when s/he professes repeatedly that they have repented of their sin and have no desire to be unfaithful in any way.

As I drive around from office to office all day in my job as a drug rep I have plenty of time to think about things. I think about what I know about what Thomas was involved in and it rips me apart. I think of how he went on a supposed errand and was actually meeting the stripper for a drink. I think of how he deceived me and planned his meeting with her, *intending* to deceive me. I think of how he sat next to me in the car and on the beach and at the table, all the while thinking of meeting with her. I think of how he must have primped in front of the mirror, cleaning himself up to see her like a teenager on a date.

I don't search for these thoughts, they come to me unbidden. They are often connected to some other memory from that time period that brings the whole mess to mind. I feel sick inside when I think on these things. It physically hurts me, and sometimes causes me to vomit. I wish I could vomit out all the memories, all the things I know about what they did together.

I have to actually shake myself to get my thoughts to change direction. I still have so many questions about things. I think knowing more would help me, and then I think it might only make things worse. I am so tired of suffering this way.

~*Mary, wife of Thomas*

Recurrent memories can be a troublesome problem for both people in the marriage as they try to move forward in the reconciliation process.

When the offended spouse struggles with recurrent memories and thoughts about their husband/wife's past sexual sin, it provides fertile ground for ongoing anger, bitterness and hurt to grow. In their thoughts and emotions, it is as though they are being sinned against over and over, keeping the hurt and betrayal alive.

The husband/wife who has repented of their sin and is demonstrating fruit of that repentance also suffers by the memories their spouse has of their sexual sin. They suffer the verbal assault of the angry outbursts and other sinful reactions when those occur. Even when there are no sinful responses, the repentant spouse sees the pain that repeatedly occurs when those memories surface. The repentant spouse relives their (forgiven) sin against their husband/wife each time it is talked through and hurt and pain is expressed.

Some days will be better than others. In the initial days after the revelation, you will be hard pressed to think or pray about anything but what has happened to you and your marriage. You might struggle getting out of bed and going on with your daily routine. One woman told me that for the first month she looked at the calendar several times each day waiting for that one month-since-I-learned-the-truth day to arrive. Each of you will pass through those first days and weeks differently; there is no "perfect" way to do this.

The Victim's Heart

The hesitation to be vulnerable again is normal in the heart of those who have been victimized because they are focused on protecting themselves from being hurt. They have been lied to and betrayed and are intent on not allowing that to happen again.

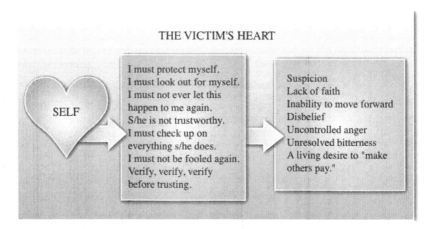

THE VICTIM'S HEART

SELF

I must protect myself.
I must look out for myself.
I must not ever let this happen to me again.
S/he is not trustworthy.
I must check up on everything s/he does.
I must not be fooled again.
Verify, verify, verify before trusting.

Suspicion
Lack of faith
Inability to move forward
Disbelief
Uncontrolled anger
Unresolved bitterness
A living desire to "make others pay."

As you look at the diagram above, note the thoughts, beliefs and desires that could flow from a heart fixated on self-preservation. Of course, not every spouse will have these specific thoughts, but in general this kind of thinking prevails.

These thoughts and beliefs lead to the behaviors you see in the second box. This is an unfortunate and ongoing consequence of sexual sin in a marriage. If it is allowed to continue, it is sure to destroy the new foundations of the marriage and relationship that are being built.

I have seen this play out over and over in numerous relationships that are attempting to reconcile after sexual sin has taken place, and it is sorrowful to behold.

When there is little trust:

- The victim is suspicious of the one who hurt them and ever-watchful—almost predatory like of the other person.
- The victim is suspicious of many of the actions of the offender.
- The victim is suspect of the motives of the offender.
- The victim perceives that the offender is always plotting and scheming some new way to hurt them.
- The victim is often irrational about the actions of the offender
- The victim seeks to demonize the offender in every respect.

When this thinking is allowed to continue unchallenged, or when the offended spouse refuses to move forward and build trust, the relationship will most likely fail. What happens is that the two people essentially switch roles and the one who was a victim becomes the offender. Counselee's Shawn and Tina were a case in point of what can happen when the offender confesses his/her sin and repents of it, but their actions are perceived as "not enough" by the victim.

Shawn had been involved in internet pornography for many years of their marriage. He had promised to stop each time she caught him. He had been practicing accountability with a man from church for the past year and Tina was sure he had overcome the problem.

One afternoon Tina learned that Shawn had again been secretly viewing pornography on the internet and renting DVD's. Her trust was shattered. She considered this adultery and everything about her husband was now in question. She told him he was a liar, cheater, adulterer, pervert, untrustworthy, purveyor of illicit sex, and a whoremonger.

Shawn sought biblical counseling and through the counseling process Shawn experienced true heart change. He confessed his sin to God, and confessed to Tina his sin against her and asked her forgiveness. He began to live out the changes in his heart on a daily basis.

Tina had been down Apology Lane before with Shawn, more times than she could remember. She was not at all sure this was for real and even told the counselor that she didn't know why this time would be any different. She did not trust Shawn's words or his new actions. She was always looking to catch Shawn in some act of deception. She was critical of his professions of change and it showed in everything she said and did concerning Shawn.

Tina, the once-victim, often perceived herself as the righteous, wounded party. She had adopted a position of self-righteousness and her pride in that was evident. She believed that Shawn was not as spiritual or as acceptable to God as she was. She communicated through verbal and non-verbal communication that she had no sin, or certainly none as egregious as Shawn's, and almost literally peered down her nose at her spouse, **"The Sinner."** This was displayed in ongoing bitterness, hard heartedness, critical spirit, condemnation, and in general, a "raising the bar" lifestyle. Whatever changes were made, whatever accountability was in place, however many hoops Shawn jumped through it was never good enough. Tina was *always* looking for that one shred of evidence to prove to herself, the counselor, their friends, but most especially to *Shawn* that he hadn't changed one little bit.

Tina needed to be confronted about her sinful attitudes toward her husband and called to account on numerous levels. What was quickly evident in this case and others like it is that while Shawn was responsible for the sin that brought this couple to the table, God used it to reveal some areas in Tina's heart that needed to be dealt with also.

What I have learned through ministering to people like Tina and Shawn, is that it quickly becomes evident that on some level—and I am not always sure they realize it—the former-victim-turned-offender (Tina) enjoys the grilling the other person gets because it validates their anger and bitterness toward them for these (in some cases) long standing sins.

Likewise, the former-offender-turned-victim (Shawn) is realizing that they are not necessarily the scum of the earth they have been made out to be since they repented of their sin!

Often, someone like Tina comes to counseling with the expectation that the former offender (Shawn) be the only one challenged, rebuked, and corrected because, in her mind, he is the only one who is in need of any kind of change! She will most likely be very offended when confronted about her sin, revealing her heart's beliefs by saying things like, "This is not why we are here," "Why are you picking on me?" and "What about him?"

This position of self-righteousness leaves little room for examination of her own heart and little room for accepting any responsibility or contribution to the problems that led up to the violations. There will be some admission that "I am not perfect either," but there is much more concern toward pointing out their spouse's wrongs. When challenged in the counseling process, the responses often begin with, "Yes, but he...." And, "Well, I did (blank) and she ...." in an attempt to shift any blame away from themselves.

In situations where someone like Tina will say she forgives, I see another common issue arise: the demand for "love" and "understanding" for how long it is taking to get over the offense. This is displayed by radical mood swings, crying jags, silent treatment, and reminders of the past offenses of which she is quick to assure him he is forgiven!

The demands for love and understanding and time to heal are often impossible to meet because no matter how much love, time, and understanding is given, it is never enough! The former offender (Shawn) is forever held as an emotional hostage by his deeds of the past.

These responses are often confusing to the former offender. For example, things at home may be going just fine; they may have enjoyed the day of companionship and then, out of the blue, the victim (Tina) suddenly becomes angry and nearly hostile toward their spouse. Sometimes no amount of asking or pleading will pry from their lips what happened. Their questions and attempts to understand are met with silence or responses like, "You should know!" or "If you loved me, you would know!"

Intimacy is mostly non-existent between the two. There will be no intimacy because she is not going to allow herself to be vulnerable again. Her heart becomes a closed room to him.

Small and insignificant matters balloon into major confrontations, and there is little peace in the home. Over time every word and deed is analyzed and becomes cannon fodder for arguments that degenerate into hostility on both sides.

If there are children involved, the victim may enlist the support of the children against the offender. I would say this is especially true in situations of sexual sin. Because the victim experiences betrayal on such an intimate level, s/he strikes out to ruin the children's opinion of their spouse.

Observation has taught me that usually by the time we get to a married couple round table, the original offender has repented and started to demonstrate the good fruit of that repentance. S/he is confused as to why things in the marriage are still going so badly overall and why their spouse reacts and responds the way they do.

The challenge in any of these situations is to move beyond the thinking of the victim mentality, cease being the offender, and go forward in a restored relationship.

CHAPTER 15

Grieving the Loss

Fellow biblical counselor Dr. Robert Kellemen has made a great impact on me and on my counseling methodology in the area of suffering. The idea of "sufferology" is his, as are many of the concepts I bring forth in this chapter.

Sufferology 101

Something to remember is that you are grieving a real loss and this will take time. His/her repentance does not eliminate the necessity of the passage of time in the healing of your heart or your marriage. One of the worst things you could do is to pretend everything is all right, because it is not.

Sometimes the grief can feel unbearable.

The Hebrew Old Testament uses more than 20 words for *grief* and *grieve*. We find examples in the Old Testament narratives of Job, Hagar (Genesis 21:17–20), Hannah (1 Samuel 1), David (2 Samuel 18:9–33) and in the New Testament in the response of Jesus to the death of Lazarus (John 11).

To say that Christians should not grieve is a ridiculous statement, yet I have been told it is said to those looking for help after experiencing loss of this kind. That is cruel and amounts to telling someone who is suffering to "get over it." However, we are not to grieve as those who have no hope. We know that Christ has come to comfort those who mourn.

David was very familiar with the feelings of abandonment in times of grief. Take a prayerful look at Psalm 88 and read the words of his soul. In those 18 verses, David grasps what it feels like to be left alone in misery and sorrow. Many of the Psalms are written by those in the midst of grief and sorrow. Take comfort in them, lose yourself in them, and pray them to God when your own words fail you.

More than anything, understand that grieving marital purity and fidelity is a *process*. It is not a marathon; it is not a race of any kind.

You cannot hurry this along, expecting to advance through phases or stages of grieving like clockwork. Grief is an intensely personal road to walk upon.

If the spouse who has committed the sexual sin finds this process difficult and is anxious to move forward, I would caution them to remember that they have grievously sinned against their spouse and have broken a sacred trust, violated the marriage covenant, and become untrustworthy in many ways. Their actions have victimized the person they pledged to honor and love until death.

Don't shrink back from the reality of your grief; it is alright to experience it. In his book, *God's Healing for Life's Losses*, Dr. Kellemen says that Candor (being honest with myself) is the first biblical response to grief.

It is a great sorrow to me to realize that some counselors diminish the importance of addressing the grief involved with sexual immorality. While self-pity is not the correct response, neither is pretending there is no pain involved. The feelings evoked by a spouse's sexual sin cannot be glossed over or ignored; they must be dealt with biblically.

Some choose to enlist the help of a counselor or pastor. There is value in such a relationship. Many Christians are not confident in their ability to address the multitude of issues that arise in such a case. Sometimes it is not so much the counsel or advice that is offered, but the knowledge that there is a caring person to help them be aware of the pitfalls of sinful responses.

There is a special burden associated with privately addressing sexual sin of this magnitude. Grieving can be complicated by dealing with the sexual sin privately, as many do. Many individuals or couples fear being ridiculed or ostracized because of the kind of sin with which they are dealing, preferring to keep the public face while aching inside.

Whether you choose to go ahead with support or alone, do not fall into the trap of denying to God or yourself that you are in the midst of true grief. There is nothing to be gained by stoicism. If your spouse is at all grieved about or repentant of their sexual sin do not deny your grief to him/her either. The reality is that a person experiences loss on multiple levels when they learn of sexual sin by their husband or wife. There is the loss of trust, the loss of security, the loss of true oneness, the loss of openness, and the loss of confidence that you really know them.

One woman told me that there is a loss of innocence and freedom in her marriage and so many things are weighted down with a heavy blanket of sorrow.

Another said she grieved deeply as she observed the easy confidence other women had about leaving their husbands for the weekend. She said that his pornography addiction stole that from her, because she would be wondering what he was doing the whole time she was gone.

My wife committed adultery and lied about it, even when I confronted her face to face. When I eventually learned the truth I felt so betrayed! I lived a lie with this woman for a year and a half of our marriage. Everything I thought was reality was fake because she was living a lie and covering up the truth. She repented and we have slowly put things back together again, but it is not the same. I used to trust her completely. She is the person I am supposed to be "one" with, but I do not trust her anymore. I live with ongoing anxiety and I am afraid to trust in what I see, because I did that before and it WAS NOT REAL. I don't want to be a fool again...I don't want to be hurt again.

I live with a burden inside that I cannot reveal to anyone. I carry a dark secret that if it were exposed would ruin my business, many lives, our reputations, and my family. Revealing this truth would shatter the carefully constructed reality I have maintained these past months. I feel like I am living a terrible lie, but the reality is that my wife has confessed her sin to me and asked my forgiveness. She has truly forsaken her sin and strives to show me she is a different person.

I am very thankful for that, but I live daily with guilt and fear.

~Kiley, husband of Adele

Kellemen lists the second biblical response in grieving as complaint. This looks like pouring out your heart to Him—all the grief, loss, anger, and heartache you carry. He is completely aware of it all because He is an all-knowing God. Christ understands because He too was betrayed and abused. He was slandered, He was maligned in character, and He was sold out for a price by someone who claimed to love Him. He intimately knows your suffering.

Share your heart with God . . . the good, the bad and the ugly. Don't fear His response, but look to Scripture for your example in biblical complaint. The Prophet Jeremiah uses very honest language in speaking to God.

> *Why do You forget us forever? Why do You forsake us so long?*
> *Lamentations 5:20*

> *O LORD, You have deceived me and I was deceived; You have overcome me and prevailed. I have become a laughingstock all day long; Everyone mocks me.*
> *Jeremiah 20:7*

> *Be gracious to me, O LORD, for I am pining away; Heal me, O LORD, for my bones are dismayed. And my soul is greatly dismayed; But You, O LORD—how long?*
> *Psalms 6:2–3*

> *For my life is full of troubles, and death draws near.*
> *Psalm 88:3 (NLT)*

> *You have thrown me into the lowest pit, into the darkest depths.*
> *Psalm 88:6 (NLT)*

He already knows your heart! Put your grief into words. Verbalize it to Him! He longs to hear the depths of your heart.

Be mindful of the difference between biblical complaint and bitter complaining. Biblical complaint desires to understand and know God in the midst of difficult circumstances. It is a request or appeal to God to help us understand Him more as we endure suffering.

Bitter complaining is full of self-pity and anger toward God. It reeks of bitterness and accuses God of being unloving and unfaithful. Complaining refuses to believe God and His promises and has as the only goal the relief of suffering at any cost.

God's plans for us often include experiencing pain and suffering. Pain always hurts no matter how we want to spiritualize it. Biblical Complaint that moves into crying out to God in your grief is the correct and third response in this process.

"Crying empties us so there is more room in us for God."[33]

You may already know that you are unable to handle this time in your life alone. You are not autonomous and you cannot be self-sufficient. In Christ you are going to have to become God-sufficient. This is a burden you cannot bear alone.

As you cling to the cross for sufficiency to redeem you, you must also keep it central in your grieving. You must direct your thoughts to the Lord and ask Him to help you to not only endure, but to grow and increase your faith and trust in Him. Ask Him to teach you about Himself and about who you are to Him.

Crying out to Him is evidence of the faith you already have in God! It is expressed confidence that you believe in the God who hears you.

> *Come and hear, all who fear God,*
> *And I will tell of what He has done for my soul.*
> *I cried to Him with my mouth,*
> *And He was extolled with my tongue.*
> *If I regard wickedness in my heart,*
> *The Lord will not hear;*
> *But certainly God has heard;*
> *He has given heed to the voice of my prayer.*
> *Blessed be God,*

Who has not turned away my prayer
Nor His lovingkindness from me.   Psalm 66:16—20

Our Loving Lord listens when we cry out to Him. He is the Shepherd of His people (Psalm 23).

You will receive help in your time of need, says the Lord (Hebrews 4:16). The help we often visualize is not what we often receive. For many, help looks like relief from the pain of betrayal, going back in time and avoiding this altogether, or having a spouse who can be completely trusted again.

God's idea of help and good are different than ours by necessity. The reality is that the end of grieving or sorrow may not be the best thing for you right now. You can be assured that God is doing some of His best work in your heart as you grapple with these things day by day. He is building things in you that may not be visible for months or years, but slowly He is transforming you into someone who will more closely resemble Christ through all of this emotional pain. Kellemen says this is when God comes to us in comfort. God's comfort may look much different than you think.

You are being touched by God in a way that is unique to your own spiritual needs and defects. Just as Jacob was touched by God

---

I am learning so much about myself. I never knew how much I actually worshipped Amy. She was the center of my universe and when her relationship with Doug came to light it was as though I had no reason to go on living.

I didn't realize then I had made her a god, someone to be worshiped and adored at any cost. I was so furious with God for allowing her to do this to me—to us—in the beginning. I see now that my relationship with God was very dependent on what He did for me. As long as things were going well in my life I was alright with God. When Amy's emotional adultery was exposed I saw how very self-focused my heart was. I was worshiping and serving God for my sake, not for His glory.

                                        ~Greg, husband of Amy

(Genesis 32) and carried a limp for the rest of his days, you too will bear the mark of God on your life from this time. He is using your suffering to purify your heart. You are in the midst of literal divine intervention as God is teaching you to voice your grief, to cry out to Him from the Scriptures, depend on Him rather than yourself, and is exposing unbelief and self-worship that lurks in your heart.

Beyond the emotional wringer of this situation, you will most likely be physically exhausted much of the time. There is a lot of emotional energy being expended in all of this. Do be gentle with yourself by getting extra sleep when you can, eating well, and spending as much time as possible in the Word of God.

Even when all the relational pieces come together, you will have periods where you are just sad. These will come and go with less frequency between them. You will find yourself beginning to live a more normal life, thinking more clearly, making plans, and actually living your life again only to return to anger, despair, biblical complaint, or self-pity. As you move forward in the grieving to healing process the times between returning to the sorrow will be further apart and you will even find yourself experiencing "normal."

Even in the midst of good days there are going to be reminders. As much as you both want to put it out of your minds forever, there are going to be

> I knew I was better when I stopped stiffening up with every text message that came into her phone. In the early days I would look at her call logs to see who she had been talking to or texting. Each time I found nothing suspicious my confidence grew a little that maybe we were going to make it.
>
> *~Mike, husband of Grace*

> I started making plans for a vacation and it hit me like a ton of bricks . . . I was making plans! It was the first time in months I could remember thinking about the future without that black cloud moving into my head reminding me what Dan had done to me. I was so excited!
>
> *~Anya, wife of Dan*

reminders. In our sex drenched culture where infidelity and promiscuity are now the social norm, you would have to live in virtual isolation to escape reminders of sexual sin.

Intrusive thoughts make it more challenging to remain forgiving. When you forgive, intrusive thoughts become a cross you choose to bear. For the one who has sinned sexually, watching you suffer is an ongoing consequence.

Put Off the old Manner of Life

The Westminster Catechism states that man's chief end is to glorify God and enjoy Him forever. When a person is burdened in their thought life, their thoughts become self-focused. They cease to honor God in their thinking and become fixated on finding relief from their pain.

To a limited extent, it is understandable that you are focusing on yourself; you have sustained a life-threatening wound to the heart. You are in deep emotional pain and pain naturally leads a person to focus on self. You want to heal; you want a break from the relentless battle in your soul.

However, even when a person is a victim, an extended self-focus does not glorify God, for it fosters idolatry of self, worships a relief from pain and freedom from the past. It promotes escapism in a variety of ways, none of which glorify God.

I understand you are in the midst of hurt, pain and anguish. I am not so cruel or heartless as to tell you to "buck up" or "get over it." I would be remiss if I did not encourage you to quell your self-focus in order to focus on Someone who is greater than yourself and your situation.

> *In reference to your former manner of life, you lay aside the old self, which is being corrupted in accordance with the lusts of deceit . . .*
> Ephesians 4:22

Self-focus equates to self-worship; for the Christian, this is unacceptable. God says we shall have no other gods before Him.

Relief, freedom and peace can become powerful gods, and we can be deceived enough to be blind to their presence in our lives.

You can put off old thoughts of the past that remind you of the pain in a manner that is not denial or without pretending they don't exist by asking the Lord to help you overcome these thoughts. Because He desires your thoughts to honor and glorify Himself, He will help you to change. If you recognize as a result of reading through this section that you have been ruminating on the hurtful thoughts instead of rejecting them, then confession to God is appropriate as well.

The memories that you struggle with produce thoughts that evoke emotional responses that tempt you to sin, so you must learn what those thoughts are in order to address them biblically. One action step that will begin to reveal the contents of your heart would be to start keeping a thought journal.

The Thought Journal[34] can be a very helpful tool for understanding your thought processes. Once you learn to recognize the thinking that leads to your emotions, you can begin to correct it by putting off those kinds of thoughts and thinking biblically.

Begin to write out the thoughts that trouble you in your thought journal. To be clear, I am not suggesting you write out your *feelings*, although sometimes it can be helpful to use your feelings and work backwards to the thoughts. Your thought journal will expose your temptations to sin in thought, word, and action.

You are not helping yourself or your spouse by going over and over the details of the sin.

When a couple sees how out of order things are biblically, they may wonder if it is too late to fix their marriage. God is sovereign over our choices and decisions and He allowed you to marry one another.

With God, there are no mistakes and He designed marriage to be for a lifetime.

Others say there is "too much damage." Often after a sexual sin or years of neglect, a spouse may believe there is just too much damage to repair. This is not true; you belong to a God who specializes in the impossible.

The same God who parted the Red Sea and raised the dead is still active in the lives of people.

If you are willing to do the hard work of growth and change and are committed to the radical amputation of sinful habits that have thrived in your marriage to this point, then there is a chance.

Even if you don't feel love for your spouse anymore, by God's grace, you can grow to love him/her again. It is so important that you understand that love is not exclusively a feeling. Feelings of love will come from acts of love.

Meditate on this TRUTH: You can change; your marriage can be transformed; it may not be too late.

You must be forward looking. Realize there is nothing you can do to change the past damage that has been done to your marriage. No amount of self-condemnation up will change anything that has happened.

Begin to tell yourself the truth when thoughts come forth about the past sexual sin. If your spouse has repented, remind yourself of that fact. You may have to remind yourself you have forgiven him/her. You have made a renewed commitment to move forward in your marriage. You want to live for the future and not in the past, so you must demonstrate self-control over your thinking.

CHAPTER 16

An Issue of Trust

Insecurity Abounds—I don't trust you anymore

You are in the midst of a trial that has broken the trust you once had in your husband/wife. Regardless of what kind of sexual sin she/he was involved in, the faith and confidence you once had for him/her has been damaged or, at the worst, destroyed.

You may wonder if *anything* s/he tells you is the truth and it may be that way for a long time. This breeds insecurity and causes you to be fearful and suspicious all the time.

> *The wise woman builds her house, but the foolish tears it down with her own hands.*   Proverbs 14:1

This proverb is also applicable to men in the sense that a person can destroy what relationship is left through fear, anger, bitterness and suspicion.

Some women check up on their husbands constantly. Some husbands, whose wives have been unfaithful, have also taken to following her via her cell phone locator device.

Insecurity in the heart is revealed by these kinds of actions and can lead to feelings of hopelessness. May I gently remind you that your security is not to be in another person, but in the Lord? Placing all your security in a changeable and fallible human is setting yourself up to be destroyed all over again.

> *The LORD is my rock and my fortress and my deliverer, my God, my rock, in whom I take refuge; my shield and the horn of my salvation, my stronghold.*   Psalm 18:2

> *God is our refuge and strength, a very present help in trouble. Therefore we will not fear, though the earth should change and though the mountains slip into the heart of the sea;*

though its waters roar and foam, though the mountains quake
at its swelling pride.   Psalm 46:1-3

It is critical that you place your spouse and your marriage into the hands of the Lord, and entrust yourself to Him as well.

Despite your fear and insecurity, you can give your repentant spouse opportunities to regain your trust.

The Trust Bank

When our children were little and began to want a little freedom to go to a neighbor's house to play or to be dropped off to see a movie with friends, we began to explain to them the idea of The Trust Bank.

We told them that their Trust Account with us was full, that they had all the trust we could have in them at that point, and where the balance in the Trust Account would be after this outing was completely up to them. They could add to their account by being exactly where they told us they would be, by doing what they told us they would do, and by coming home on time. This would give them greater potential to receive approval for larger or "riskier" things like sleep overs and out of town events in the future.

If our children came home late, or we learned they had been dishonest with us, the result was a withdrawal from their Trust Account. This meant that there would be more restrictive measures taken for a while until they regained our trust.

The key was that they were not sent to their room for 3 months, but that they had an opportunity to regain our trust again through small and structured steps that were designed to help them succeed. We also adopted the "trust but verify" method. Our kids knew that we would check up to see if they were really where they'd said they would be.

Now, of course some of this is not applicable in a marriage, but the idea can be utilized nonetheless. You, as the wounded and betrayed spouse, must allow your husband/wife to regain your trust through testing in life situations.

Some spouses work together on ways to make this happen such as giving full access to their computer, not erasing computer history logs, and installing special software that will let an accountability partner see where they have been and what searches have been done on the internet. Others require a phone call when leaving work and driving home and financial accountability for every dime spent.

The day will come when you will simply have to trust that your husband/wife is being faithful and true to you. The more little trust building opportunities that are behind you, the easier this will be. You will need to entrust your spouse and your marriage to the Lord and remind yourself that if your husband/wife proves not to be trustworthy, the greater violation is against God, not you.

Keeping the Godward perspective is imperative; therefore, I suggest routinely reading Psalms and Proverbs to gain wisdom, insight and understanding.

Because deception is such an integral aspect of sexual sin, the temptation is to disbelieve everything your spouse tells you. It is easy for someone to tell you to just believe him or her because they are not in your marriage and they don't feel your heartbreak. They also don't live with your fears regarding deception.

> I have a hard time believing anything he tells me anymore. While he says he has repented, I am not sure I believe him. In my head I think, "Oh, really? Well, we'll see about that." I keep waiting for him to reveal something he has been hiding from me all this time even though he has told me over and over that he is through with her. He tells me all the time that he loves me and that he is so glad to be done with all that sin and secrecy, and as much as I *want* to believe him...I am not always sure I do. I keep waiting for him to accidentally say her name when he tells me he loves me instead of mine. It is a hard way to live.
>
> ~Patty, wife of Willis

It is not biblical for you to continually disbelieve your spouse if you have agreed to remain in the marriage and have determined to forgive him/her. You may not realize it, but each time you do not accept his/her words as truth you are accusing him/her of being a liar. In the above example, Patty did not understand that the more she told herself that he was untrustworthy, the more she convinced herself it was still true.

This makes it very difficult to move forward and rebuild trust in the marriage. My encouragement to you is to accept what is told to you as the truth and pray that the Lord would confirm it for you as truth or a lie. God detests lying as much as all other sin, and He exposes the things done in the darkness.

Building trust will come with the passage of time. The more your spouse has proven to be honest with you, the more you will find trust beginning to build. This will not be accomplished overnight but will come a little at a time.

Your spouse should understand this process, patiently waiting for you to see the changes that are taking place in his/her heart.

Pray, Don't Ruminate
1 Thessalonians 5:17 says to "pray without ceasing." You are undoubtedly in one of the most difficult, if not *the* most difficult, time of your life. Prayer must be constant if you are going to spiritually thrive in the midst of this trial.

Prayer will help you to cultivate a dependence on God in every circumstance of your life. Praying without ceasing means you pray with repetition and pray often; you have an ongoing conversation with the Lord either audibly or silently in the privacy of your heart.

Ruminating is a repeated and fairly constant focus on the pain you are enduring. Yes, prayer can be an aspect of ruminating because it can sometimes mean meditation. However, I am not using the word in a positive way here. Ruminating in this case would mean you are repeatedly thinking about the sin that has been committed against you and reciting over and over to God how what s/he did makes you feel.

Just as a cow chews the cud, ruminating is repeatedly allowing your mind to entertain thoughts that you know will cause you emotional pain. When you ruminate there is no moving forward, there is little healing taking place, and you perpetuate the pain you so badly want to escape.

To avoid ruminating, ask the Lord to help you delight in Him alone. God is intentional and purposeful in all He allows into our lives and He has fashioned this trial to accomplish things in you that could not and would not have been accomplished any other way.

> God has done a very great work in my soul in the middle of this personal disaster. My counselor told me that this time is "intentional and purposeful" and that God is using it to help me become more like Jesus.
>
> I realize that I placed too much on my husband; I see now that I actually worshipped him and that I thought he was above this kind of sin. I had to see him for the fallen man he really is and not as some super-saint. God is the only One who can really be my all in all. While all this is overwhelmingly painful, I would not trade what I am learning for anything.
>
> ~Grace, wife of Max

The Lord seeks a deeper relationship with you, one that is above the love you have with your husband/wife. He has your attention now. Use this time wisely to increase the amount and intensity of your prayer life.

Prayer is something we are all called to do, but it seems that it takes a crisis of this magnitude for the Lord to get the attention of some people. It is possible that circumstances are very painful for you right now, so prayer comes easy. There is much to bring before the Lord as you and your spouse move forward. Your prayer life may never have been more vibrant.

You will be tempted to do nothing but pray about your marriage and your pain. There is, of course, a place for that, but your prayer life must go beyond this. I would encourage you to pray what you find in God's Word—pray the Psalms and pray God's words back to Him.

Pray for the needs of others! Getting your eyes off of your own situation is necessary. There is no better way to cultivate a heart of thankfulness than to pray for other people's problems and needs. Seeing the trials other people are going through can help you understand how gracious God is toward you, even though you are suffering in this time.

You will be amazed at how these little steps can make such a difference in your heart and life and in the relationships you have struggled with for so long. You don't need to avenge yourself or be afraid of being made a fool. God, who sees and knows all, will honor your desire to follow Him and to honor Him by how you live.

What about sex?

> Once I knew about the adultery, I did not think I could live with him anymore. Knowing about the pornography was bad enough, but he assured me he had stopped that several years ago and I believed him. I was ready to leave and go back to my parent's house.
>
> I could not imagine allowing him to ever touch me again, not after he touched that whore and allowed her to touch him. I was so tormented by the thoughts of him saying to her the things he said to me in our intimate moments that I didn't think I would ever be able to have sex with him again.
>
> *~Karen, wife of Allen*

Reintroducing sex into your marriage will be a very, very individual thing. There is no timetable to follow for intimacy so do not allow someone to push or cajole you into resuming sexual relations before you are ready to do so. I have seen some very negative outcomes when one spouse is pressured into sex before s/he is ready.

To be clear, Scripture states it is ungodly for a married couple to withhold themselves from the sexual relations aspect of marriage.

> *Now concerning the things about which you wrote, it is good for a man not to touch a woman. But because of immoralities, each man is to have his own wife, and each woman is to have her own husband. The husband must fulfill his duty to his wife, and likewise also the wife to her husband. The wife does not have authority over her own body, but the husband does; and likewise also the husband does not have authority over his own body, but the wife does. Stop depriving one another, except by agreement for a time, so that you may devote yourselves to prayer, and come together again so that Satan will not tempt you because of your lack of self-control.* 1 Corinthians 7:1—5

The key in this case is to agree to **wait and pray**. Ask for the Lord's help with this area of your marriage, for Him to work in your spouse's heart, bringing them to the place where s/he will desire to be intimate again.

Because I knew many of the sexual acts they did with one another I was so determined not to do or have done the things they did together. He constantly assured me that he regretted what he had done, that he was stupid and foolish to have ever strayed.

He told me he would wait for me to be ready, and that he would not push me. I was so thankful for that! He told me many times a day that he was praying for me; praying that God would heal me and help me to deal with his sin. He prayed God would help me to truly forgive him, and admitted he did not deserve my forgiveness.

I know I was not responsible for any of his sin, he was; but I didn't want to contribute to temptation for him by refusing sex.

~Karen

Many women whose husbands have been sexually immoral struggle with intrusive thoughts during sex. Whether it is comparing their body to those of the porn actresses or the daring actions of his former lover, women have a hard time not reacting to such thoughts. Some have said they pictured their husband with the other woman, or visualized imaginary scenes between the two of them. They have had accusing and negative thoughts about themselves during sexually intimate interludes. I have been told by some wives that they have burst into tears, had a panic attack, and become very angry during or right after sex.

Good communication is essential to overcome these emotional responses. Part of your counseling agenda must be to deal with your thoughts, beliefs, and responses toward sex and toward your spouse. Be willing to be as honest as possible with your spouse, speaking the truth in love, of course, and let him/her know your thoughts and fears. Remember, the goal is to move forward. In every sense of the word you will be moving forward and progressing into a new marriage with your husband/wife.

As I've previously said, your thought life will play a major role in holding you back or helping you move forward.

...I talked a lot about how I was struggling with havingsex with him for many years. I was always comparing myself to the girls in his movies and those magazines I would find, and I felt so inadequate! My body did not look llike any of those girls and never would; I am just so... average in every way.

When I thought about having sex with Allen again, it just made my stomach hurt. Now, I not only had the porn girls to contend with, but a real live woman withwhom he had been having sex! Who would he be seeing in his mind while he wasphysically having sex with me? It took me weeks to overcome those thoughts and to re-mind myself of all he said to me since he repented, how much he hated what he had done, and how sick and disgusted he was by his former behavior.

As my counselor taught me, I spoke truth to myself about the present. I cannot change the past, but what I do today will affect the future. I want to honor God and I want to be Allen's wife.

I did have some very difficult moments our first time. I had to stop and take deep breaths and just collect myself. Allen was very patient, and I could tell he felt so bad as he watched my struggles.

To be honest, the first few months were just me going through the motions in many ways. I wanted Allen, but I was not able to reach satisfaction because my thoughts kept getting in the way. I would picture them together, or think of something he told me about their time together and I would just lose it.

In a way, I was reclaiming what was mine. I decided I was not going to let that horrible woman ruin the rest of my life. Allen was my husband; he stayed with me. Rather than looking at all the years the locusts had eaten, I became determined to do what I could to make a better future for us.

~Karen

Karen was deeply, deeply hurt by my infidelity. I knew I was not worthy of such a wonderful woman and that God had simply blessed me by giving her to me. I knew I had squandered many years and deprived myself of a godly helpmeet by my sinful foolishness.

I could not believe she was willing to stay with me, let alone have sex with me again.

I was determined not to hurt her again, so I went with the pace she set for intimacy. I wanted her to begin to trust me; most of all, I wanted her to see I was finally worthy of her trust.

It crushed me how she cried and cried and fought for every ounce of composure she could muster up when we first started having sex again.

> I knew how hard it was for her; it was written all over her face.
>
> Her actions toward me and the undeserved love she has shown me have been a wonderful picture of God's love for me and all sinners. None of us deserve His love and I know I don't deserve her love either.
>
> *~Allen*

Karen and Allen represent what we hope the outcome will be for every couple who weathers this storm of life. They concluded counseling individually and as a couple and returned to what they called "real life" about 1 year after Allen's adultery was discovered.

Shortly after the one year mark they held a Marriage Recommitment Ceremony in their church. They wrote new vows and made a new marriage covenant before God.

No, things won't be the same as they were before the sexual sin, but they can be better.

> *Then I will make up to you for the years that the swarming locust has eaten.* Joel 2:25a

CHAPTER 17
Moving Forward: Alone

Not every couple is like Allen and Karen. It would be wonderful if every sinner would repent and change and if every spouse would be willing to honor God by forgiving and moving forward with their spouse in life.

If you did not want the divorce, or you divorced because your spouse abandoned you, your response to being single will be very different than that of the person who wanted it. I assume that because you are reading this book, you are the spouse who really did not want to end the marriage; there was just no real option to continue in it.

The reality is that in many Bible believing churches divorce is allowed in cases of adultery and abandonment. If you have taken the divorce option or you have been divorced by your spouse, you are facing a far different future than the one you planned on when you said, "I do."

When you married, you and your spouse were one flesh, united by God. When you are divorced, it is a literal rending of something that was once whole. It is emotionally painful, and can devastate virtually every area of your life.

Shock, numbness, grief, fear, and a host of other emotions may now be a consistent part of your days and nights. You experience moments where you just burst into tears, or wish you could. When a couple divorces, there are so many violent changes that take place and change often inspires fear. Financial changes are what incite the most fear in men and women involved in divorce.

Financially, divorce is expensive and depending on where you live, you may bear part or all of the legal fees.

Women who have stayed home or worked small non-skilled jobs may find themselves suddenly having to provide for their own food, clothing and shelter. You may have to find a job that will offer benefits and retirement, and if you have been out of the workplace for any number of years that may be a daunting task.

You have most likely been uprooted from your home either because you could not afford to buy out your spouse or could not afford to maintain it with all the other expenses you now face alone. There will be penalties and cancellation fees that accompany the closure of accounts and disconnection of services in the middle of contracts as part of the home sale.

If you have children, their lives have also been uprooted and their pain and confusion add an excruciating dimension to this situation. Visitation schedules and split holidays, as well as having two homes and parents with two very different lives, are circumstances children of divorce have to learn to cope with.

Grieving[35]

Many people are familiar with the Kubler-Ross approach to grief and suffering. It is originally described as a five-stage process that those facing death and dying go through. Later it was amended to include those experiencing any kind of major loss including loss of a job, a divorce, adultery, abandonment and so on. I do not find the Kubler-Ross stages to be particularly helpful; none of those stages are found in the Bible, yet they are normal, human responses to tragic suffering.

Another area that may cause grief is the thought of being alone for the rest of your life. If your spouse has a significant other, it is especially difficult to bear the sudden aloneness of divorce. Both men and women express concern for their futures and what will happen to them later in life if they remain unmarried.

Many people, as well meaning as they are, have no idea how to address a person who is grieving a divorce or abandonment. When a death takes place, those mourning gather together at the funeral or memorial to comfort the ones who have suffered the immediate loss; and to some degree, they get comfort for themselves. However, once the funeral is over, the comfort of others usually disappears after a week or two and you are left alone. The cards stop coming, the meals cease, and the phone calls end. You are even expected to resume your job duties after mourning for a mere three days! (Personally, I find that barbaric.)

There is no three-day allowance for the death of hopes and dreams in a marriage. There is no funeral when a marriage dies. Few people are insightful enough to understand that empty, hollow, terrifying feeling that comes when you wonder every minute of the day what your former spouse is doing in your absence.

Some people have said that death is easier than divorce. For everyone else, life goes on as it did before. Perhaps there is an empty place at the card table, or a seat to be filled at the ball game. But when a marriage blows apart, especially due to sexual sin, a man or woman loses someone they loved and with whom shared their life. The ex-husband or wife has moved on to a new life and a new living situation and has left their former spouse with the wreckage of the old life.

The people on the fringes of the life of a divorcee have no idea how to relate to them after the truth comes out. Many are callous and crude and tell the person how lucky they are to be rid of the scum. They may even suggest you throw yourself a party when the ink on the divorce paper is dry.

Others will say nothing because they fear that bringing up the loss will cause you to be sad and sorrowful all over again.

You may appear to be doing well, have your "game face" on, but inside you are deeply, mortally wounded. To some degree people know that. Whether you realize it or not, this is one reason some people appear to be uncomfortable around you. They don't want to cause you to cry or hurt, so in many cases they say nothing about your loss with the exception of asking how you are doing. No one wants to say the wrong thing, so they may appear to be insensitive, hurrying you on through the grief process by suggesting you begin to date again or that you can somehow "pay back" your spouse for his/her treachery.

If you appear to be falling apart, your friends and co-workers might suggest you attend a support group. There are a few popular groups I know about and most of them deal with felt needs. I think support groups can be helpful when the focus of the group is on the resources we have in Christ. However, experience has shown that overall these kinds of groups are fertile ground for anger, bitterness, slander and replaying the tragedies and sin committed against the group attenders over and over. I also think that support groups tend to foster the idea that no one else can understand my pain except those who are in my situation.

Those who want to remarry and are biblically allowed to do so find themselves thrust into a much different dating scenario than the one they left for marriage.

Those who struggle with the dating scene or are not outgoing may experience loneliness. There is sometimes a sense of not fitting in anymore; churches are made of families and many single people comment on feeling left out. This adds to an already great sense of isolation.

All of these issues bring a tremendous temptation to succumb to fear, worry, and anxiety. This is one of the many reasons I suggest you continue to receive biblical counseling. As you transition into this new phase of life, you will come against things that you may need help working through in a manner that glorifies God.

This passage has been helpful to many people who have been divorced or abandoned by their spouse.

> *"Fear not, for you will not be put to shame;*
> *And do not feel humiliated, for you will not be disgraced;*
> *But you will forget the shame of your youth,*
> *And the reproach of your widowhood you will remember no more.*
> *For your husband is your Maker,*
> *Whose name is the LORD of hosts;*
> *And your Redeemer is the Holy One of Israel,*
> *Who is called the God of all the earth.*
> *For the LORD has called you,*
> *Like a wife forsaken and grieved in spirit,*
> *Even like a wife of one's youth when she is rejected,"*
> *Says your God.*

"For a brief moment I forsook you,
But with great compassion I will gather you.
In an outburst of anger
I hid My face from you for a moment,
But with everlasting lovingkindness I will have compassion on
you,"
Says the LORD your Redeemer.

Isaiah 54:4—8

The greatest relationship for you to cultivate is the one you have with the Lord. He will always love you and will never forsake you. I suggest you use this time in your life to grow deeper and more mature in your faith.

CHAPTER 18
Final Thoughts

When we began this walk together I told you that despite what your husband/wife has done, I wanted you to understand that adultery and other sexual sin does not have to ruin your life or your marriage. Sexual sin does not define who you are. Along the way you have read the stories of people like you—broken and sin-sick people who have been searching for hope, healing, and help during a devastating time in life.

To conclude our journey together, I want to direct your focus toward the big picture. To properly interpret life, you must always have the Big Picture—the Biggest Picture—in view. All of life is meant for the glory of God alone. Please do not allow the details of your life, personal relationship, or spouse's sexual sin to cause you to lose sight of the only important thing: Jesus Christ. In every conversation you have with your spouse, it is His honor and His glory which you are to desire.

Allow me to encourage you to look past the person and the problems that have led you to read this book and to see Jesus Christ. He is the "one thing needed" in every circumstance.

There are redemptive purposes in the pain you are currently in. I understand that you may just want it all to be over and to be done with all the pain and heartache that it has brought you. Instead, endeavor to cooperate with the Lord. God allows some things to cause us to desire Him more, to need Him more, and to want Him more.

Have you noticed that the times when you are suffering are often the times when you seek Him in greater measure? Through this difficult time in your life, you can come to know Jesus' comfort and peace in new ways.

It is in the dark times that you grow in grace and in the knowledge of the Lord Jesus Christ. During these times you can know for sure that there is only one thing that is needed: to have fellowship with God through His Son; that can never be taken away!

Everything that really matters is already yours in Christ. You have God's love and forgiveness and are indwelt by the Holy Spirit. He provides you with the wisdom and direction you will need to navigate the stormy seas of this life. He has sealed your justification and forever removed the stain and power of sin. You have peace with God, and grace from God; there is nothing you must do to earn it or to maintain it, for it has been done on your behalf. Nothing can separate you from His love! Nothing can destroy your life or disrupt your fellowship with Him. You can truly rejoice in the midst of difficult circumstances.

Whatever happens in this life will not steal your eternity. You have been given a never-ending destiny that is sure and certain with God in Christ. That is what matters. You must fix your eyes on the cross and the gospel.

Because of the blood of Jesus Christ you have been redeemed. Now you can worship at the throne of the King. You can call upon Him for help in this present time of need, and you are welcomed into His presence in a way that is reserved only for His children.

Remember that God is the sovereign God of the universe and He does what He wants with what is His. He has ordained this time for you and your spouse and He intends to sanctify you through it.

> *Blessed be the God and Father of our Lord Jesus Christ, the Father of mercies and God of all comfort, who comforts us in all our affliction so that we will be able to comfort those who are in any affliction with the comfort with which we ourselves are comforted by God.*   2 Corinthians 1:3—4

Amazing things can happen when a person endeavors to live their life for the glory of God, and when both husband and wife truly desire to reconcile and honor God from this point forward in their marriage. Put forth the effort in the process of biblical change, and watch the God of the Universe at work!

APPENDIX
Special Circumstances

Unfortunately, sexual sin is not always confined to consensual sex between adults. It is sad to even have to include a section such as this one. This section is dedicated to the spouse of a person who commits an illegal sexual act.

Illegal sexual acts are increasing in numbers. Men have historically been the major perpetrators against women and children; that still appears to be the case today. However, female sex offenders are increasing in number and their victims are usually adolescent boys and young men. The "cougar" mentality is currently very big in our society and there is a shocking number of teachers preying on their students and having sex with them.

The statistics for criminal sexual sin recidivism are enormous[36] and "A 2002 study by the United States Department of Justice indicated that recidivism rates among sex offenders was 5.3 percent; that is, about 1 in 19 of released sex offenders were later arrested for another sex crime."[37]

Many sex offenders act in ways that would indicate a seared conscience (considered sociopathic by the psychiatric community)—during their criminal activities they behave in ways that would violate a sensitive conscience.

There is no fear of God in such a person. Their lives are dominated by activities that make other people very uncomfortable, to state it mildly. There is little to no guilt or shame, little to no self-control, excessive lying, and a belief s/he is not accountable to anyone.

> *...there is no fear of God before their eyes.*　　　Romans 3:18

What do you do when your spouse is arrested for a crime such as rape, solicitation of a prostitute, incest, sodomy, found to be in possession of child pornography, or for soliciting a minor for sex?

Tragically, this is becoming a more frequent problem in our society and what affects society will also affect the church. It is especially difficult because in addition to facing the reality of sexual sin, the spouse is also facing the reality that their husband or wife has been involved in deviant sexual behavior.

I have had several cases over the years with wives of men who have committed sex crimes. The toll this takes on a woman and the marriage is beyond my ability to articulate. What I want you to know first is that nothing that has been done by the offender is beyond the reach of forgiveness in Christ Jesus.

That truth causes some people to become very angry because we like to rate sins in the order of their heinousness. To God, all sin is equally heinous and all sin (apart of blaspheming the Holy Spirit) is forgivable when a person repents and is regenerated.

Our obligations as Christians remain the same:

> *Preach the word; be ready in season and out of season; reprove, rebuke, exhort, with great patience and instruction.*
> *2 Timothy 4:2*

and

> *always be(ing) ready to make a defense to everyone who asks you to give an account for the hope that is in you, yet with gentleness and reverence.* *1 Peter 3:15b*

We are to preach the message of the cross to those who are perishing, and preach repentance and heart change to those who have professed Christ and yet have fallen into such deep, deep sin.

This level of sexual sin brings the need for heightened discernment in those ministering to the offender. Often there is a dulled or seared conscience (1Timothy 4:2) and learning the truth can be difficult. The counseling process can be discouraging for the counselor and the spouse because offenders are often labeled as "sex addicts" or "sociopaths," which give them a label onto which they can hold. The label can relieve them of responsibility for their actions because with the label comes a medical diagnosis code that states they have a disease or disorder.

As a practical matter, counseling people who demonstrates the actions and attitudes of what is labeled sociopathic is very challenging. These people are such effective liars and deceivers that it is very hard to discern when they are speaking truth! This makes ascertaining true biblical repentance very difficult because they can and will tell you what you want to hear and be very convincing. This causes quite a bit of uncertainty in the spouse going forward.

Legalities

When there are sex crimes there will be legalities, and when the law is involved there will be mandated programs for the sex offender that will be contrary to biblical counseling methodologies. If the offender even desires to be involved with a faith-based program it is unlikely that a biblical approach would be accepted by the courts at this point in time.

I believe that biblical counseling can be effective to address the spiritual issues that are the core of the problem; however, it will require a very great commitment on the part of the offender to participate in both programs because of the amount of homework involved in biblical counseling and the requirements the court will place upon the offender.

Cost may also be an issue, as some states and counties require the offender to pay his/her cost of treatment, and not all biblical counseling is free, either.

Loneliness

The women I have counseled who were married to sex offenders found it to be a very lonely existence. They have told me that there is really nowhere they fit in. Their families are not always supportive, and they are subjected to an ongoing barrage of criticism of the offending spouse and offered all kinds of "counsel" as to what to do with the marriage.

Adding to the loneliness is the social stigma of being married to a sex offender. This certainly can lead a spouse to isolate and withdraw from normal life. When your spouse commits a sexual assault you become known as "The Sex Offender's Wife" or the wife of the man "who did that" to someone. If you have children, the effects on them are also devastating and harmful emotionally and spiritually, if not addressed biblically.

The neighbors are fearful and don't want the offender around at all. People can be very unkind and make horrible comments to the spouse and children about the offender, or ask questions that are very embarrassing regarding personal issues.

The church may ask the woman to come to church alone if the husband is not incarcerated. In a few of the cases with which I was involved, the church body was notified of the man's arrest by announcement and through a letter mailed to the homes of the church attenders and members. This was to protect the church body and for liability reasons. Additionally, the Matthew 18 process was set in motion or finalized with the arrest or conviction. It is all very, very public.

The courts will prohibit the offender from being where women and especially children are present. Because of the offense, often the husband is not allowed to attend church or any home/small group activities, so his wife faces staying home or going alone. In some cases, with permission, the offender may be able to meet for a men's study, but only if there are no women or children on the premises at the time. Meeting in public is often prohibited for the same reasons.

If he is on house arrest pending trial or on probation, there are tremendous expenses that accompany his being in the home. Electronic monitoring devices, polygraphs and other legal obligations will add up in a hurry! It is pretty much certain he will have lost his job as a result of the arrest so the family income is cut in half or more adding more strain on an already stressful situation.

Humiliation and other emotions

I have had women tell me how humiliating it is on so many different levels to be married to a man who has committed such crimes. The temptation to sinful anger and bitterness is enormous and the wife must have constant support from her church and other godly people if she is to withstand this time in her life.

She may experience guilt and shame at her husband's actions, and wonder like nearly every other woman whose husband sins sexually why she was not enough. These can be dark and depressing days for a wife.

In the midst of all that is swirling around her the biblical admonition to forgive her husband is still there. In the face of mounting financial woes and her husband's probable prison term, many women opt to divorce and move on. Even if a woman takes the divorce option she must still forgive him before God and forgive him personally if he asks her to.

Even when he has been excommunicated and/or imprisoned, the obligation of the church to urge him to repent is still present, as well as the command to pray for him and visit him in prison.

I am sad to say we are facing much more of this type of ministry opportunity in our future; the world grows more corrupt with each passing day and sexual sin is now predominant in our world.

THOUGHT JOURNAL

The Thought Journal is intended to help you see your thoughts, beliefs, desires and feelings in an objective manner. The goal is to determine the thoughts, beliefs and desires that must change to help you move through the point where you are stuck or struggling in your heart/life.

Initially you are to include your feelings in your thought journal. Frequently, the phrase, "I feel" is used erroneously to describe what are actually thoughts, beliefs, and desires of the heart. Identifying everything as a feeling is inappropriate and will severely restrict your spiritual growth.

God has commanded us to live by faith, not by feelings. As you continue to work through this exercise you will notice your thoughts and words changing as you interact with people.

Begin to write out the thoughts that trouble you in your thought journal. To be clear, I am not suggesting you write out your *feelings*, although sometimes it can be helpful to use your feelings and work backward to the thoughts. Your thought journal will expose your temptations to sin in thought, word, and action.

Some people simply journal their day and the events that took place and put a special emphasis on their thinking and feelings.

When you see your thoughts on paper you can then determine if they are biblical and God-honoring thoughts or sinful thoughts.

Asking yourself questions will help you to address the thoughts in a manner that glorifies God.

The text of Philippians 4:4—9 outlines some of the things our thoughts are to be focused on:

> *Rejoice in the Lord always; again I will say, rejoice. Let your reasonableness be known to everyone. The Lord is at hand; do not be anxious about anything, but in everything by prayer*

and supplication with thanksgiving let your requests be made known to God. And the peace of God, which surpasses all understanding, will guard your hearts and your minds in Christ Jesus.

Finally, brothers, whatever is true, whatever is honorable, whatever is just, whatever is pure, whatever is lovely, whatever is commendable, if there is any excellence, if there is anything worthy of praise, think about these things. What you have learned and received and heard and seen in me—practice these things, and the God of peace will be with you.

Here are some questions to help you get started with analyzing your thought journal:

- Am I rejoicing in my thoughts/attitude?
- Are my thoughts focused on my circumstances?
- Are my thoughts reasonable or unreasonable? Do I have "crazy" thinking going on? Am I creating sinful scenarios in my mind?
- Am I thinking about things that are making me anxious? What things am I thinking about right now?
- Do my thoughts center on "what if" or "if only?" How does this help me? Is there truth in either of those questions?
- Are my thoughts thankful ones? What are my thankful thoughts?
- Am I praying about the things that are bothering me? What are those things specifically? Am I actually *praying* or am I ruminating and calling it prayer?
- Are my prayers focused on having things work out my way or for God's glory?
- Do I think about what is true and real or am I thinking about lies I believe about myself, others, or my circumstances?

- Are my thoughts honoring to God and others? Are they respectful or profane?
- Do I desire what is just or do I want my own way in this situation?

- Am I angry? Who or what am I angry at? Am I angry because I got something I didn't want? Am I angry because I didn't get something I wanted?
- Is my thinking pure? Do I allow my thoughts to fixate on ungodly things? Holy or unholy?
- Are my thoughts kind or gracious about others or my situation?
- Am I thinking about things that are good versus evil?
- Do my thoughts reflect an understanding of God's sovereignty in my life?
- Do my thoughts reflect an acceptance of God's sovereignty in this situation?

Writing out answers to questions such as the ones above will help you to view them objectively. Attempt to support those thoughts that you believe are justified with Scripture.

ABOUT THE AUTHOR

Julie Ganschow has been involved in Biblical Counseling and Discipleship for nearly 20 years. She ministers to women through Biblical Counseling for Women and writes a daily blog on counseling issues. She is Executive Director of Reigning Grace Counseling Center.

Her extensive training has led to certification with the Association of Certified Biblical Counselors (ACBC), the American Academy of Biblical Counselors (AABC) and the International Association of Biblical Counselors (IABC) where she functions as the State Coordinator for Missouri.

She makes her home in Kansas City, Missouri with her wonderful husband Larry, along with Buddy and Bambi, their sweet little Chihuahuas.

She is the author of numerous books and materials for biblical counseling and training. Julie is also a frequent conference speaker.

You can find her blog at www.bc4women.blogspot.com, and information about the ministry can be found at www.rgcconline.org and www.biblicalcounselingforwomen.org.

NOTES

CHAPTER 1

[1] Wayne Mack, *Strengthening Your Marriage* (Phillipsberg, NJ: P&R, 2009) 6.

[2] Bruce Roeder, "The Marriage Covenant" (lecture, Reigning Grace Counseling Ministries, Track 6 Lesson 1, West Allis, WI, 2006).

CHAPTER 2

[3] eros. Dictionary.com. Online Etymology Dictionary. Douglas Harper, Historian. http://dictionary.reference.com/browse/eros (accessed: February 12, 2009).

[4] Ibid.

[5] Deceit. Dictionary.com. http://dictionary.reference.com/browse/deceit (accessed: February 12, 2009).

CHAPTER 3

[6] Wikipedia.com, "Phone Sex" http://en.wikipedia.org/wiki/Phone_sex (accessed: February 12, 2009).

[7] N.a. "Does the Bible say Masturbation is Sin?" http://bible.org/question/does-bible-say-masturbation-sin accessed 3/27/12.

[8] N.a. "Facebook Causing a third of all divorces: UK Survey," Press Trust of India, London: May 24, 2012

CHAPTER 4

[9] Jerry Ropelato, "Internet Pornography Statistics" http://internet-filter-review.toptenreviews.com/internet-pornography-statistics.html accessed 3/27/12.

[10] Ibid.

[11] This information is anecdotal, gleaned from general conversations from a random sampling of women who have been asked over the past 20 years.

[12] Pure Life Ministries (www.purelifeministries.org) and Setting Captives Free (www.settingcaptivesfree.com) are two programs I recommend.

[13] I suggest you Google the phrase "pornography and brain damage" to review the most recent updates on this topic. While there are

always articles of little substance and subjective opinion, there is objective research that substantiates porn's harmful effects on the brain.

14 The Association of Certified Biblical Counselors (ACBC) (www.biblicalcounseling.com) and the International Association of Biblical Counselors (www.IABC.net) are two trusted sources to find a Biblical Counselor.

CHAPTER 5

15 Bruce Roeder, "A Theology of Heart Change Part 2, Mark 7:14–23" (Sermon delivered at Grace Community Church, West Allis, WI 10/08/2006), http://media.sermonaudio.com/mediapdf/1080615187.pdf accessed 2/02/07

CHAPTER 6

16 Thayer's Greek Definitions (Cedar Rapids: Parson's Technology Inc.) *Brown-Driver-Briggs' Hebrew Definitions* Electronic Edition STEP Files Copyright © 1999, FindExoduscom, Inc. All rights reserved.

17 B.t. Express *Do It ('til You're Satisfied)* lyrics by the Lyrics Bay team. Property and copyright of their actual owners. Copyright 2003-2011

CHAPTER 9

18 One such resource would be Jerry Bridge's book, *Trusting God, Even When Life Hurts* (Colorado Springs: NavPress, 1998).

CHAPTER 10

19 Arthur W. Pink *The Fruits of Repentance* http://www.the-highway.com/repent4_Pink.html accessed 12/1/12

20 John MacArthur, NKJV John MacArthur Study Bible (Thomas Nelson, 1998) footnotes on 1 Corinthians 7:10.

21 Ibid.

CHAPTER 11

22 Ropelato, Internet Pornography, http://internet-filter-review.toptenreviews.com/internet-pornography-statistics-pg5.html accessed 5/28/12

23 Ibid.

24 See chapter 2 for a review of this material.

25 John MacArthur Study Bible, NKJV Version, Notes on 1 Peter, Historical and Theological Themes, pg 1937.

26 See Chapter 1 to review.

27 I would suggest a thorough reading of the document posted here from John MacArthur's Grace to You Ministry: http://www.gty. org/resources/distinctives/dd04/divorce-and-remarriage accessed 7/9/12. I would also strongly urge a careful reading of Jay Adam's book, *Marriage, Divorce, and Remarriage in the Bible* (Grand Rapids: Zondervan, 1986). This book is very informative and I found it very helpful over the years when such cases arise.

28 John MacArthur states in his commentary section from the NKJV John MacArthur Study Bible on 1 Peter 3, "The loving, gracious submission of a Christian woman to her unsaved husband is the strongest evangelistic tool she has." For the husband he says regarding praying for his wife in a way that those prayers will not be hindered, "This refers specifically to the husband's prayer for the salvation of his wife." I would direct you to the John MacArthur Study Bible Commentary on 1, 2 Peter, regarding this passage for further clarification.

CHAPTER 12

29 John MacArthur, "Who Is an Adulterer?" Part 2, Matthew 5:27–30 (Panorama City, CA: Grace to You) May 13, 1979, accessed June 14, 2012.

30 To review, see chapter 10

CHAPTER 14

31 A sick child or elderly parent that requires care would be an exception. In general, your relationship with your spouse becomes your number one priority after your relationship with God.

32 A peace-faker dislikes controversy and avoids conflict. A typical response of a peace-faker is to avoid controversy at any cost. "Peacemakers are distinguished from peace-fakers by their willingness to candidly discuss conflicts that are too serious to overlook. This discussion may include confession and forgiveness, loving confrontation, respectful instruction or debate, and thoughtful negotiation (see Proverbs 28:13; Ephesians

4:32; Matthew 5:23—24; 18:15; John 3:1—21; 4:1-26; 2 Tim. 2:24—26; Dan. 1:1—16; Philippians 2:3—4). When differences cannot be resolved in private, peacemakers will not give up; instead, they will seek guidance from other believers and submit themselves to the counsel and discipline of the church (see Matthew 18:16-20; 1 Corinthians 6:1—8; Acts 15:1—35)." http://www.peacemaker.net/site/apps/nlnet/content2.aspx?c=aqKFLTOBIpH&b=1043497&ct=1254849, accessed 6/20/12

CHAPTER 15

[33] Robert W. Kellemen, *God's Healing for Life's Losses* (Winona Lake, IN: MBH Books, 2010) 44.

[34] Thought Journal, Appendix page 211.

CHAPTER 17

[35] As with your married counterparts, I would suggest working through a copy of *Life's Healing for Life's Losses* by Dr. Robert Kellemen.

APPENDIX-SPECIAL CIRCUMSTANCES

[36] John Ashcroft, "Recidivism of Sex Offenders Released from Prison in 1994," U.S. Department of Justice Report, Bureau of Justice Statistics, November, 2003- http://bjs.ojp.usdoj.gov/content/pub/pdf/rsorp94.pdf accessed 7/9/12.

[37] Wikipedia.com, "Sex Offender," http://en.wikipedia.org/wiki/Sex_offender#cite_note-bjs-rsorp94-1, accessed 7/9/12.

Made in the USA
San Bernardino, CA
24 September 2016